2016

中国国际收支报告

China's Balance of Payments Report

国家外汇管理局国际收支分析小组

BOP Analysis Group

State Administration of Foreign Exchange

中国金融出版社

China Financial Publishing House

责任编辑：张翠华
责任校对：孙　蕊
责任印制：裴　刚

图书在版编目（CIP）数据

2016 中国国际收支报告 (2016 Zhongguo Guoji Shouzhi Baogao)／国家外汇管理局国际
收支分析小组 . —北京：中国金融出版社，2017.6
　　ISBN 978-7-5049-9004-4

　　Ⅰ . ① 2 ⋯　Ⅱ . ①国 ⋯　Ⅲ . ①国际收支—研究报告—中国—2016
Ⅳ . ① F812.4

　　中国版本图书馆 CIP 数据核字（2017）第 096209 号

出版
发行　　**中国金融出版社**

社址　　北京市丰台区益泽路 2 号
市场开发部　　（010）63266347，63805472，63439533　（传真）
网上书店　http://www.chinafph.com　　（010）63286832，63365686　（传真）
读者服务部　　（010）66070833，62568380
邮编　　100071
经销　　新华书店
印刷　　天津银博印刷集团有限公司
尺寸　　210 毫米 ×285 毫米
印张　　12.25
字数　　192 千
版次　　2017 年 6 月第 1 版
印次　　2017 年 6 月第 1 次印刷
印数　　1—2000
定价　　80.00 元
ISBN 978-7-5049-9004-4
如出现印装错误本社负责调换　联系电话：（010）63263947

国家外汇管理局
国际收支分析小组人员名单

组　　　长：潘功胜

副 组 长：邓先宏　方上浦　杨国中　郑　薇

审　　　稿：徐卫刚　孙天琦　郭　松　张生会　崔汉忠

统　　　稿：王春英　温建东　周　济　贾　宁　韩　健　赵玉超

执　　　笔：

第一部分：李　萌　平晓冬　张青青

第二部分：陈　丰　贺　萌　胡　红　彭　星　马玉娟

第三部分：杨　灿

第四部分：梁　艳　程娅婕

第五部分：管恩杰

专　　　栏：李　萌　赵玉超　常国栋　牛保顺　王琳娜　杨　灿

附录整理：平晓冬

英文翻译：周海文　王　亮　胡　红

英文审校：Nancy Hearst（美国哈佛大学费正清东亚研究中心）

Contributors to This Report

Head
Pan Gongsheng

Deputy Head
Deng Xianhong   Fang Shangpu   Yang Guozhong   Zheng Wei

Readers
Xu Weigang   Sun Tianqi   Guo Song   Zhang Shenghui
Cui Hanzhong

Editors
Wang Chunying   Wen Jiandong   Zhou Ji   Jia Ning
Han Jian   Zhao Yuchao

Authors
Part One: Li Meng   Ping Xiaodong   Zhang Qingqing
Part Two: Chen Feng   He Meng   Hu Hong   Peng Xing   Ma Yujuan
Part Three: Yang Can
Part Four: Liang Yan   Cheng Yajie
Part Five: Guan Enjie
Boxes: Li Meng   Zhao Yuchao   Chang Guodong
        Niu Baoshun   Wang Linna   Yang Can
Appendix: Ping Xiaodong

Translators: Zhou Haiwen   Wang Liang   Hu Hong

Proofreader: Nancy Hearst (Fairbank Center for East Asian Research,
            Harvard University)

内容摘要

2016 年，全球经济复苏依然缓慢，国际金融市场波动加剧；我国经济总体缓中趋稳、稳中向好，经济运行保持在合理区间。

2016 年，经常账户顺差仍处于合理水平。全年顺差 1 964 亿美元，与 GDP 之比为 1.8%。其中，货物贸易顺差与 GDP 之比为 4.4%，服务贸易逆差与 GDP 之比为 2.2%。跨境资本流出压力总体有所缓解。2016 年，非储备性质的金融账户逆差 4 170 亿美元，较上年下降 4%。一方面，境内主体境外资金运用的方式更加多元化，对外直接投资、证券投资和其他投资均呈增长态势，对外资产合计净增加 6 611 亿美元。另一方面，境内主体偿还对外负债告一段落，跨境融资需求回升，境内主体对外负债由净流出转为净流入。2016 年，外国来华直接投资、证券投资和其他投资等外来投资净流入 2 441 亿美元，上年为净流出 1 010 亿美元。

2017 年，预计我国经常账户将保持一定规模顺差，与 GDP 之比继续处于合理区间；资本和金融账户（不含储备资产）逆差有望收窄，虽然外部环境中的不稳定、不确定因素依然较多，但国内经济平稳运行、对外投资更趋理性、金融市场对外开放逐步深化等积极因素也会继续发挥作用。外汇管理将按照稳中求进的工作总基调，兼顾便利化和防风险。一方面，继续扩大金融市场开放，提升贸易投资便利化水平，服务实体经济发展；另一方面，加强外汇市场监管，维护良好的外汇市场秩序，防范跨境资本流动风险。

Abstract

In 2016, the global economy was recovering slowly, with increasing fluctuations in international financial markets. The Chinese economy registered slower but stable performance, with a good momentum for growth, and it was operating in an acceptable zone.

A reasonable current account surplus was recorded, totaling USD 196.4 billion and accounting for 1.8 percent of GDP. In particular, the ratio of the surplus of trade in goods to GDP was 4.4 percent, and the ratio of trade in services to GDP was 2.2 percent. Pressures from cross–border capital outflows were generally alleviated. In 2016, the deficit in the non–reserve financial account totaled USD 417 billion, down by 4 percent. On the one hand, domestic entities were investing in overseas markets via numerous channels. Outward direct investments, portfolio investments, as well as other investments all increased, which together led to a net increase of USD 661.1 billion in external assets. On the other hand, external debt payments by domestic entities slowed down and their need for cross–border financing rebounded, which led to net inflows instead of net outflows under the external debt item. In 2016, inward investments, including FDI, portfolio investments, and other investments achieved a net inflow of USD 244.1 billion. In 2015, they recorded a net outflow of USD 101 billion.

In 2017, the current account is expected to maintain a surplus, with the ratio to GDP within a reasonable level. The deficit in the capital and financial account (excluding reserve assets) is expected to decrease. Despite unstable and uncertain factors in the external environment, positive factors, such as a stable domestic economy, more rational overseas investments, and amore intensive opening up of the financial market, will also play a role. The SAFE will make progress while ensuring stability and taking into account both convenience and risk prevention. It will further the opening up of the financial market and improve trade and investment facilities to serve economic development. In addition, the SAFE will strengthen regulation of the foreign–exchange market to maintain proper discipline against risks of cross–border capital flows.

目 录

专栏

图

表

Content

Boxes

Charts

Tables

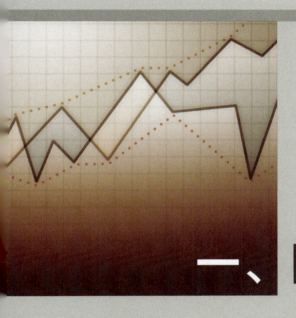

一、国际收支概况

（一）国际收支运行环境

2016 年，我国面临错综复杂的内外部经济金融形势：世界经济缓慢复苏，国际经济政治领域的不确定性因素增多，主要发达经济体货币政策进一步分化；国内经济运行总体平稳，但结构性矛盾仍较突出。

世界经济缓慢复苏。 美国经济形势相对较好，但大选之后未来政策走向尚不明朗；欧元区经济略有改善，但仍面临难民问题、银行业风险等；日本经济复苏缓慢且缺少政策空间；英国经济在公投脱欧后总体稳定，但脱欧安排仍有较大不确定性。新兴市场经济体有所企稳，但仍面临调整与转型压力（见图 1-1）。根据国际货币基金组织（IMF）2017 年 1 月《世界经济展望》预测，2016 年发达经济体和新兴市场经济体的经济增长预计分别为 1.6% 和 4.1%，较 2015 年分别下降 0.5 个百分点和持平。

全球货币政策继续分化。 2016 年 12 月 14 日，美联储宣布将联邦基金利率目标区间上调 25 个基点至 0.5%~0.75%，同时仍预计宏观经济复苏状态将使加息以渐进方式进行。为刺激经济和提振通胀，欧央行于 2016 年 3 月 10 日加大量化宽松货币政策力度，下调多个指标利率并扩大资产购买规模和范围，此后又相继推出若干宽松措施。日本央行于 2016 年 1 月 29 日实施超预期负利率政策，引入三级利率体系，将金融机构存放在日本央行的部分超额准备金利率从 0.1% 降至 −0.1%。英格兰银行

图 1-1

主要经济体经济增长率

注：美国数据为季度环比折年率，其他经济体数据为季度同比。
数据来源：环亚经济数据库。

2016 年上半年维持基准利率和资产购买规模不变，公投脱欧后决定实施一揽子刺激措施，下调基准利率并增加资产购买规模。新兴经济体货币政策持续分化，一方面，俄罗斯、印度、巴西、韩国等国为提振经济、缓解外部冲击，均连续调低指标利率，另一方面，南非、哥伦比亚、埃及和墨西哥等国收紧货币政策，以应对国内通胀压力和美联储加息的冲击。

国际金融市场波动性上升。2016 年，全球政治经济社会领域"黑天鹅"事件频现，民粹主义、逆全球化、贸易及投资保护主义抬头，地缘政治不确定性上升，加剧金融市场波动。2016 年，美元指数上涨，日元对美元升值，欧元和英镑对美元贬值，多数新兴市场货币对美元贬值；主要经济体国债收益率继续分化，全球股市普遍回升，大宗商品市场有所回暖，美国道琼斯工业平均指数、欧元区斯托克 50 指数和 MSCI 新兴市场股指分别上涨 13.4%、0.7% 和 8.6%，S&P GSCI 商品价格指数上涨 27.8%（见图 1-2 和图 1-3）。

国内经济运行总体平稳。2016 年，我国经济运行缓中趋稳、稳中向好，供给侧结构性改革取得进展，国内生产总值（GDP）达到 74.4 万亿元，增长 6.7%，居民消费价格（CPI）上涨 2%（见图 1-4），就业形势基本稳定。经济增长质量继续改善，

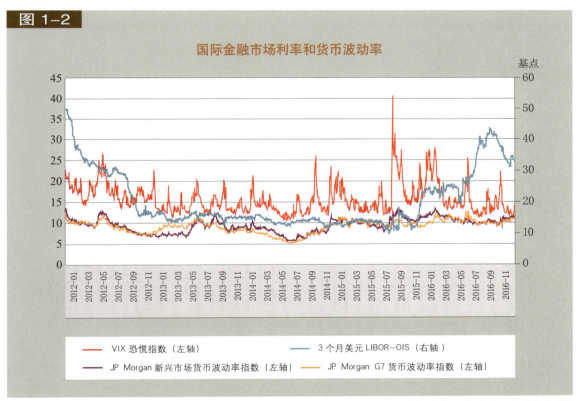

图 1-2

国际金融市场利率和货币波动率

VIX 恐慌指数（左轴）　　3 个月美元 LIBOR-OIS（右轴）
JP Morgan 新兴市场货币波动率指数（左轴）　　JP Morgan G7 货币波动率指数（左轴）

注：BEMS 和 BGSV 分别为彭博新兴市场和发达国家主权债券指数，MXEF 为 MSCI 新兴市场股指，SPX 为美国标准普尔 500 股指，SX5E 为欧元区斯托克 50 股指，SPGSCI 为标准普尔 GSCI 商品价格指数，均以 2012 年初值为 100。
数据来源：彭博资讯。

图 1-3

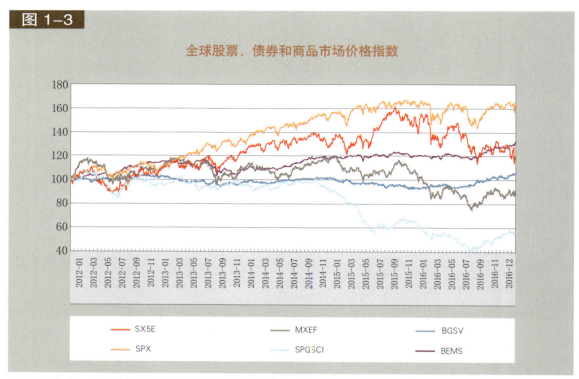

全球股票、债券和商品市场价格指数

注：BEMS 和 BGSV 分别为彭博新兴市场和发达国家主权债券指数，MXEF 为 MSCI 新兴市场股指，SPX 为美国标准普尔 500 股指，SX5E 为欧元区斯托克 50 股指，SPGSCI 为标准普尔 GSCI 商品价格指数，均以 2012 年初值为 100。
数据来源：彭博资讯。

图 1-4

季度 GDP 和月度 CPI 同比增长率

数据来源：国家统计局。

服务业在国内生产总值（GDP）中的比重增长到 52%，消费对经济增长的贡献率为 62%，新兴业态消费增长较快。2016 年，我国继续实施稳健的货币政策，根据形势发展变化，保持政策灵活适度，注重稳定市场预期，为供给侧结构性改革营造了适宜的货币金融环境。但也必须看到，我国经济结构性矛盾仍较突出，民间投资活力尚显不足，内生增长动力仍待加强，稳定经济增长、防范资产泡沫和促进环境保护之间的平衡还面临较多挑战。

专栏 1

推改革、促平衡的效果逐步显现

面对复杂多变的外汇市场形势，人民银行、外汇局牢牢抓住改革的有利时间窗口，按照既有利于眼前，平衡外汇收支和防范跨境资本流动风险，又有利于长远，推动金融市场开放和资本项目可兑换的原则，侧重推动扩大流入端的政策改革，在扩大改革开放，服务实体经济的同时，有力地促进了国际收支平衡，维护了外汇市场供求关系稳定。

一是推动银行间债券市场对外开放，资本项目可兑换水平迈上新台阶。2016 年 2 月，发布中国人民银行公告 [2016] 第 3 号，进一步拓宽境外机构投资者范围，便利更多类型的境外机构投资者依法合规投资银行间债券市场。2016 年 5 月，对境外机构投资者实行登记管理，不设单家机构限额或总限额，规定资金汇出入币种基本一致，避免资金大进大出对国际收支平衡的冲击。截至 2016 年 12 月底，已有 180 家境外机构 / 基金在上海总部注册备案，进一步提高了银行间债券市场对外开放水平；2016 年 3 月以来，非居民持有的境内债券资产余额总体上升，截至年末市值达到 8 700 亿元人民币（见图 C1-1），更好地满足市场主体利用国际国内"两个市场"、"两种资源"。

二是全面实施全口径跨境融资宏观审慎管理，便利市场主体跨境融资。建立健全宏观审慎框架下的外债和资本流动管理体系，是"十三五"规划的重要部署，是深化外汇管理改革、促进投融资便利化的重要举措。2016 年 1 月，允许 27 家试点金融机构和注册在四个自贸区的企业在与其资本或净资产挂钩的跨境融资上限内自主开展本外币跨境融资。2016 年 5 月，在总结前期试点经验的基础上，将全口径跨境融资宏观审慎管理政策推广全国，缓解企业"融资难、融资贵"问题。自 2016 年第二季度起，我国本外币外债余额止跌回升（见图 C1-2）。

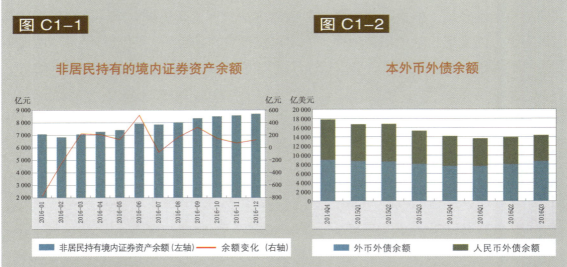

图 C1-1

非居民持有的境内证券资产余额

图 C1-2

本外币外债余额

数据来源：国家外汇管理局。

三是深化合格境外机构投资者外汇管理改革，营造良好的外商投资环境。2016 年 2 月和 8 月，分别实施合格境外机构投资者（QFII）和人民币合格境外机构投资者（RQFII）外汇管理改革，放宽单家机构投资额度上限、简化审批管理、便利资金汇出入、放宽锁定期限制，提高对 RQFII 和 QFII 外汇管理的一致性，进一步推动境内资本市场开放。政策实施后，为跨境证券投资提供了更多便利，促进了市场主体跨境投融资的便利化。截至 2016 年 12 月末，共有 278 家 QFII 机构获批合计 873 亿美元额度，177 家 RQFII 机构获批合计 5 285 亿元人民币额度。

四是改革和规范资本项目结汇管理方式，平衡外汇市场供求关系。2016 年 6 月，全面实施外债资金意愿结汇管理，统一境内机构资本项目外汇收入意愿结汇政策，大幅缩减资本项目收入及结汇用途负面清单，进一步满足和便利境内企业经营与资金运作需要，便利市场主体跨境投融资。

（二）国际收支主要状况

2016 年，经常账户顺差 1 964 亿美元，较上年下降 35%；非储备性质的金融账户逆差 4 170 亿美元，下降 4%（见表 1-1）。

表 1-1 中国国际收支差额主要构成　　　　　　　　　　　单位：亿美元，%

项　目	2010 年	2011 年	2012 年	2013 年	2014 年	2015 年	2016 年
经常账户差额	2 378	1 361	2 154	1 482	2 360	3 042	1 964
与 GDP 之比	3.9	1.8	2.5	1.5	2.3	2.7	1.8
非储备性质的金融账户差额	2 822	2 600	−360	3 430	−514	−4 345	−4 170
与 GDP 之比	4.6	3.4	−0.4	3.6	−0.5	−3.9	−3.7

数据来源：国家外汇管理局、国家统计局。

货物贸易保持较大顺差。按国际收支统计口径[①]，2016 年，我国货物贸易出口 19 895 亿美元，进口 14 954 亿美元，分别较上年下降 7% 和 5%；顺差 4 941 亿美元，虽然较上年的历史高位下降 14%，但仍显著高于 2014 年度及以前各年度水平。

服务贸易逆差增长趋缓。2016 年，服务贸易收入 2 084 亿美元，较上年下降 4%；支出 4 526 亿美元，增长 4%；逆差 2 442 亿美元，增长 12%。其中，旅行项下逆差 2 167 亿美元，增长 6%，增幅较上年下降 6 个百分点（见图 1-5）。

初次收入[②]延续逆差。2016 年，初次收入项下收入 2 258 亿美元，较上年增长 1%；支出 2 698 亿美元，增长 2%；逆差 440 亿美元，增长 7%。其中，雇员报酬顺差 207 亿美元，较上年下降 25%；投资收益逆差 650 亿美元，下降 6%（见图 1-5）。从投资收益看，我国对外投资的收益为 1 984 亿美元，增长 5%；外国来华投资利润利息、股息红利等 2 634 亿美元，增长 2%。

二次收入逆差收窄。2016 年，二次收入项下收入 309 亿美元，较上年下降 14%；支出 404 亿美元，下降 17%；逆差 95 亿美元，下降 25%（见图 1-5）。

直接投资转为逆差。按国际收支统计口径，2016 年，直接投资[③]逆差 466 亿美元，上年为顺差 681 亿美元（见图 1-6）。其中，直接投资资产净增加 2 172 亿美元，较上年多增 25%；直接投资负债净增加 1 706 亿美元，较上年少增 30%。

证券投资逆差收窄。2016 年，证券投资逆差 622 亿美元，较上年下降 6%（见图 1-6）。其中，我国对外证券投资净流出 1 034 亿美元，增长 41%；境外对我国证券投资净流入 412 亿美元，增长 512%。

---

　　① 本口径与海关口径的主要差异在于：一是国际收支中的货物只记录所有权发生了转移的货物（如一般贸易、进料加工贸易等贸易方式的货物），所有权未发生转移的货物（如来料加工或出料加工贸易）不纳入货物统计，而纳入服务贸易统计；二是计价方面，国际收支统计要求进出口货值均按离岸价格记录，海关出口货值为离岸价格，但进口货值为到岸价格，因此国际收支统计从海关进口货值中调出国际运保费支出，并纳入服务贸易统计；三是补充部分进出口退运等数据；四是补充了海关未统计的转手买卖下的货物净出口数据。

　　② 国际货币基金组织《国际收支和国际投资头寸手册》（第六版）将经常项下的"收益"名称改为"初次收入"，将"经常转移"名称改为"二次收入"。

　　③ 本口径与商务部公布的数据主要差异在于，国际收支统计中还包括了外商投资企业的未分配利润、已分配未汇出利润、盈余公积、股东贷款、金融机构吸收外资、非居民购买不动产等内容。

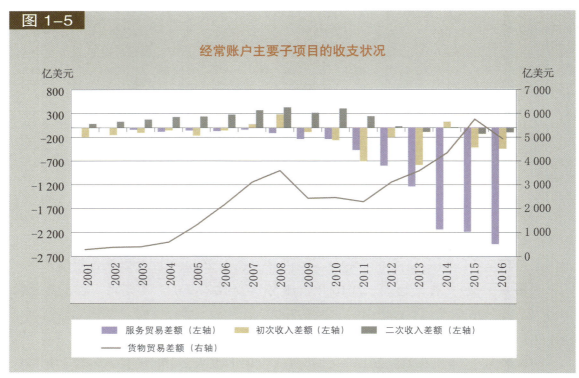

图 1-5

经常账户主要子项目的收支状况

数据来源：国家外汇管理局。

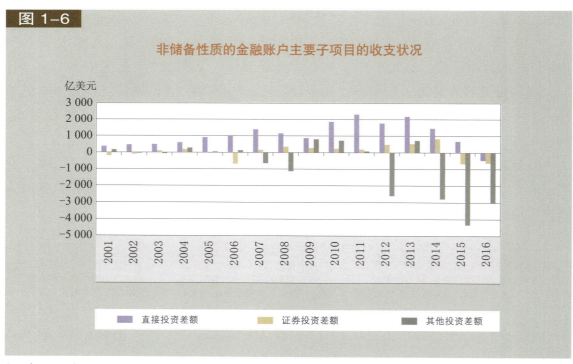

图 1-6

非储备性质的金融账户主要子项目的收支状况

数据来源：国家外汇管理局。

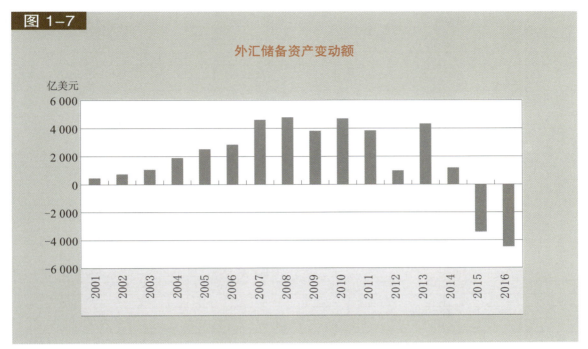

图 1-7

外汇储备资产变动额

数据来源：国家外汇管理局。

其他投资逆差明显下降。 2016 年，贷款、贸易信贷和资金存放等其他投资逆差3 035 亿美元，较上年下降 30%（见图 1-6）。其中，我国对外的其他投资净增加3 336 亿美元，增长 305%；境外对我国的其他投资净增加 301 亿美元，上年为净减少 3 515 亿美元。

储备资产继续下降。 2016 年，我国交易形成的储备资产（剔除汇率、价格等非交易价值变动影响）减少 4 437 亿美元。其中，交易形成的外汇储备资产减少 4 487亿美元（见图 1-7）。截至 2016 年末，我国外汇储备余额 30 105 亿美元。

表 1-2　2016 年中国国际收支平衡表

单位：亿美元

项　　目	行次	2016 年
1．经常账户	1	1 964
贷方	2	24 546
借方	3	−22 583
1.A 货物和服务	4	2 499
贷方	5	21 979
借方	6	−19 480
1.A.a 货物	7	4 941
贷方	8	19 895
借方	9	−14 954
1.A.b 服务	10	−2 442
贷方	11	2 084
借方	12	−4 526
1.A.b.1 加工服务	13	184
贷方	14	185
借方	15	−2

项　　目	行次	2016 年
1.A.b.2　维护和维修服务	16	32
贷方	17	52
借方	18	−20
1.A.b.3　运输	19	−468
贷方	20	338
借方	21	−806
1.A.b.4　旅行	22	−2 167
贷方	23	444
借方	24	−2 611
1.A.b.5　建设	25	42
贷方	26	127
借方	27	−85
1.A.b.6　保险和养老金服务	28	−88
贷方	29	41
借方	30	−129
1.A.b.7　金融服务	31	11
贷方	32	32
借方	33	−20
1.A.b.8　知识产权使用费	34	−228
贷方	35	12
借方	36	−240
1.A.b.9　电信、计算机和信息服务	37	127
贷方	38	254
借方	39	−127
1.A.b.10　其他商业服务	40	147
贷方	41	580
借方	42	−432
1.A.b.11　个人、文化和娱乐服务	43	−14
贷方	44	7
借方	45	−21
1.A.b.12　别处未提及的政府服务	46	−20
贷方	47	12
借方	48	−32
1.B　初次收入	49	−440
贷方	50	2 258
借方	51	−2 698
1.B.1　雇员报酬	52	207
贷方	53	269
借方	54	−62
1.B.2　投资收益	55	−650
贷方	56	1 984
借方	57	−2 634
1.B.3　其他初次收入	58	3
贷方	59	6
借方	60	−2
1.C　二次收入	61	−95
贷方	62	309
借方	63	−404
2. 资本和金融账户	64	263
2.1　资本账户	65	−3
贷方	66	3
借方	67	−7
2.2　金融账户	68	267
资产	69	−2 174
负债	70	2 441
2.2.1　非储备性质的金融账户	71	−4 170
资产	72	−6 611
负债	73	2 441
2.2.1.1　直接投资	74	−466
2.2.1.1.1　直接投资资产	75	−2 172
2.2.1.1.1.1　股权	76	−1 484

续表

项　目	行次	2016 年
2.2.1.1.1.2 关联企业债务	77	−688
2.2.1.1.2 直接投资负债	78	1 706
2.2.1.1.2.1 股权	79	1 642
2.2.1.1.2.2 关联企业债务	80	64
2.2.1.2 证券投资	81	−622
2.2.1.2.1 资产	82	−1 034
2.2.1.2.1.1 股权	83	−385
2.2.1.2.1.2 债券	84	−649
2.2.1.2.2 负债	85	412
2.2.1.2.2.1 股权	86	189
2.2.1.2.2.2 债券	87	223
2.2.1.3 金融衍生工具	88	−47
2.2.1.3.1 资产	89	−69
2.2.1.3.2 负债	90	22
2.2.1.4 其他投资	91	−3 035
2.2.1.4.1 资产	92	−3 336
2.2.1.4.1.1 其他股权	93	0
2.2.1.4.1.2 货币和存款	94	−435
2.2.1.4.1.3 贷款	95	−1 147
2.2.1.4.1.4 保险和养老金	96	−3
2.2.1.4.1.5 贸易信贷	97	−1 008
2.2.1.4.1.6 其他	98	−743
2.2.1.4.2 负债	99	301
2.2.1.4.2.1 其他股权	100	0
2.2.1.4.2.2 货币和存款	101	102
2.2.1.4.2.3 贷款	102	−196
2.2.1.4.2.4 保险和养老金	103	−6
2.2.1.4.2.5 贸易信贷	104	162
2.2.1.4.2.6 其他	105	239
2.2.1.4.2.7 特别提款权	106	0
2.2.2 储备资产	107	4 437
2.2.2.1 货币黄金	108	0
2.2.2.2 特别提款权	109	3
2.2.2.3 在国际货币基金组织的储备头寸	110	−53
2.2.2.4 外汇储备	111	4 487
2.2.2.5 其他储备资产	112	0
3. 净误差与遗漏	113	−2 227

注：1. 本表根据《国际收支和国际投资头寸手册》（第六版）编制。
　　2. "贷方"按正值列示，"借方"按负值列示，差额等于"贷方"加上"借方"。本表除标注"贷方"和"借方"的项目外，其他项目均指差额。
　　3. 本表计数采用四舍五入原则。
数据来源：国家外汇管理局。

（三）国际收支运行评价

经常账户顺差仍然处于合理区间。 2016 年，我国经常账户顺差与 GDP 之比为 1.8%，较上年下降 0.9 个百分点，依然处于合理水平。其中，货物贸易顺差与 GDP 之比为 4.4%，下降 0.8 个百分点；服务贸易逆差与 GDP 之比为 2.2%，增加 0.2 个百分点；初次收入和二次收入合计逆差与 GDP 之比为 0.5%（见图 1-8）。

跨境资本流出压力总体有所缓解。 2016 年，非储备性质的金融账户逆差 4 170 亿美元，较上年下降 4%。其中，第一季度，非储备性质的金融账户逆差 1 263 亿美元，较上年第四季度的 1 504 亿美元下降 16%；第二季度，非储备性质的金融账户逆差大幅收窄至 524 亿美元；第三季度逆差反弹到 1 351 亿美元，为 2016 年的季度

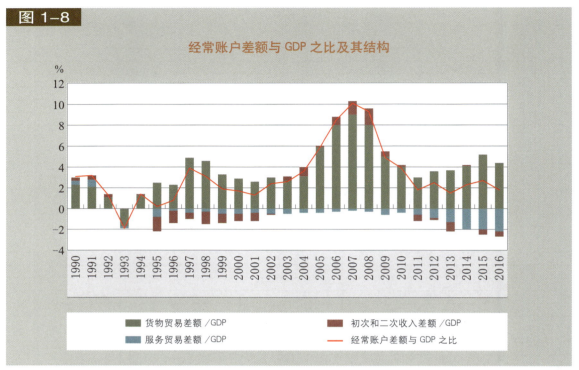

图 1-8

经常账户差额与 GDP 之比及其结构

数据来源：国家外汇管理局、国家统计局。

图 1-9

国际收支差额与外汇储备资产变动

数据来源：国家外汇管理局。

逆差最高值，但仍明显低于 2015 年第三、第四季度的逆差规模；第四季度，非储备性质的金融账户逆差收敛至 1 031 亿美元，同比下降 31%（见图 1-9）。

境内市场主体继续增持境外资产。 2016 年，境内主体境外资金运用的方式更加多元化，对外直接投资、证券投资和其他投资均呈现增加态势，对外资产合计净增加 6 611 亿美元，较上年多增 98%。其中，对外直接投资净增加 2 172 亿美元，多增 25%，占全部对外投资净增加额的 33%，较上年占比下降 19 个百分点；对外证券投资净流出 1 034 亿美元，多增 41%，占比为 16%，较上年占比下降 6 个百分点；对外存款、贷款等其他投资净增加 3 336 亿美元，多增 305%，占比为 50%，较上年占比增加 25 个百分点（见图 1-10）。

境内机构境外负债由净流出转为净流入。 2016 年，外国来华直接投资、证券投资和其他投资等外来投资净流入（即对外负债净增加）2 441 亿美元，上年为净流出 1 010 亿美元。其中，第一季度净流出 135 亿美元，第二季度起转为净流入并逐季上升，分别为 771 亿美元、842 亿美元和 963 亿美元（见图 1-11）。首先，直接投资项下境外资本继续保持一定规模净流入，全年净流入 1 706 亿美元，其中下半年为 958 亿美元，较上半年增长 28%；其次，来华证券投资净流入 412 亿美元，较上年增长 512%，体现了我国证券市场对外吸引力的增强以及开放度的加深；再次，来华其他投资净流入 301 亿美元，上年为净流出 3 515 亿美元，说明境内主体偿还境外负债告一段落，跨境融资需求回升。

图 1-10

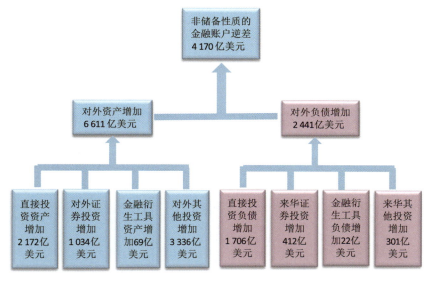

2016 年中国跨境资本流动的结构分析

数据来源：国家外汇管理局。

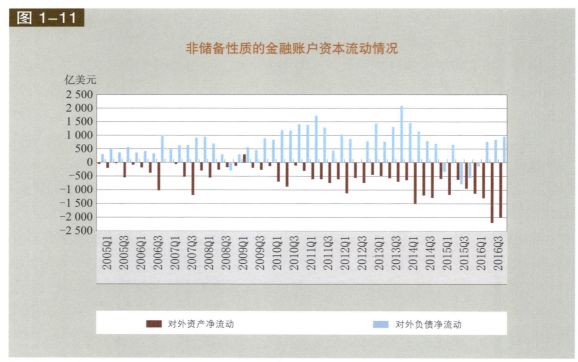

图 1-11

非储备性质的金融账户资本流动情况

亿美元

■ 对外资产净流动　　　■ 对外负债净流动

数据来源：国家外汇管理局。

当前我国跨境资本流出压力主要来自境内，总体风险依然可控。2016年，我国外债恢复净流入，跨境资本流出主要表现为境内主体增持对外资产，包括对外直接投资、证券投资、贷款等多种方式。2014—2016年，我国各类对外投资合计增加近1.5万亿美元，相当于2013年之前8年的累计规模，2016年更是达到6 611亿美元。上述变化总体上体现了我国综合国力和企业实力的提升，反映了境内主体多元化资产配置的需求，但境内市场主体对外资产增长较快，对我国国际收支的短期影响较大，其中也存在一些非理性和异常的投资行为。总体来看，由于我国经济增速在世界范围内仍处于较高水平、财政状况相对良好、金融体系总体稳健、经常账户持续顺差和外汇储备依然充裕，因此，我国国际收支风险总体可控，能够抵御和逐步适应境内主体对外资产的调整，但也需高度关注、积极防范相关风险。

专栏2

客观看待当前我国外汇储备规模及其变动

截至2016年末，我国外汇储备余额30 105亿美元，尽管已从峰值回落，但目前规模仍处于较高水平，相关变动也需要客观看待。

　　当前我国外汇储备规模在世界范围内依然高居榜首。从 2016 年末全球各国（地区）的外汇储备相对规模看，我国稳居首位。第二位日本为 1.16 万亿美元，第三位瑞士为 6 349 亿美元，巴西、印度、俄罗斯均为 3 000 多亿美元（见图 C2-1）。在全球 10.7 万亿美元的外汇储备规模中，我国占 28%，日本和瑞士分别占 11% 和 6%。

图 C2-1

外汇储备规模前十位国家（地区）

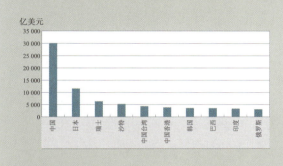

图 C2-2

主要国家（地区）外汇储备占比（%）

　　从对外支付能力和债务清偿能力看，我国外汇储备仍十分充裕。目前，全球无公认统一的标准衡量储备充足度。按照传统的衡量标准，在进口支付方面，外汇储备至少需要满足 3 个月的进口，假定没有人民币对外支付，目前为 4 000 亿美元左右的外汇需求。在对外债务偿还方面，外汇储备需要覆盖 100% 的短期外债，目前的本外币短期外债规模为八九千亿美元，比 2014 年末的 1.3 万亿美元明显下降，说明近一段时期我国外债偿还压力已得到较大释放。因此，总的来说，从当前我国的外汇储备规模看，国际支付和清偿能力依然很强，能够很好地维护国家经济金融安全。

　　从外汇储备满足境内主体增持对外资产需求的角度看，储备变化本质上反映了我国对外资产持有主体的结构变化，是一个逐步发展的过程，也具有积极意义。近年来，随着我国企业、个人经济实力的增强，我国民间部门多元化配置资产的需求相应增加。从国际投资头寸表看，截至 2016 年末，我国民间部门对外资产占全部对外资产的比重首次过半，达到 52%，民间部门对外资产和对外负债的匹配度趋向改善。2016 年末，我国民间部门对外净负债

1.3 万亿美元，较 2014 年末的 2.3 万亿美元高点明显下降。而且，满足民间部门增持对外资产需求不一定全靠外汇储备。我国经常账户持续顺差，跨境融资、市场开放等政策也便利了境外资金流入，这些都可以成为境内主体增加对外资产的资金来源。当然，对外资产在官方和民间部门之间的调整需要合理、适度，与国家的经济发展水平、对外开放程度相协调。未来我国将在增强汇率弹性的同时保持人民币汇率在合理均衡水平上的基本稳定，不断健全宏观审慎管理框架下的跨境资本流动管理体系，这都有利于相关调整平稳进行。

近期外汇储备变动也反映了官方外汇市场操作、储备资产价格变动和储备的多元化运用等因素。具体来看：一是央行在外汇市场的操作，一方面满足我国市场主体对外直接投资、证券投资、贷款等各类投资需求，2014 下半年以来上述投资增加超过 1.2 万亿美元；另一方面用于证券投资以及外债等其他投资资金流出，2014 下半年以来净流出 2 700 多亿美元，其中，2016 年第二季度以前累计净流出 4 000 亿美元左右，第二季度以来转为净流入近 1 300 亿美元。二是外汇储备投资资产的价格波动，也会导致储备余额发生变化。三是由于美元作为外汇储备的计量货币，其他各种货币相对美元的汇率变动可能导致外汇储备规模的变化。四是根据国际货币基金组织关于外汇储备的定义，外汇储备在支持"走出去"等方面的资金运用记账时会从外汇储备规模内调整至规模外，反之亦然。

二、国际收支主要
项目分析

（一）货物贸易

货物贸易进出口总额降幅收窄，外贸依存度持续下降。 据海关统计，2016 年，我国出口较上年下降 8%，进口下降 5%；进出口总额 3.7 万亿美元，下降 7%，较上年降幅收窄了 1.3 个百分点；进出口顺差 5 107 亿美元，下降 14%。2016 年，我国外贸依存度（即进出口总额 /GDP）为 33%，较上年下降 3 个百分点，连续 6 年下降（见图 2-1）。

进口和出口数量均上升，进口价格逐步由降转升。 2016 年，国内需求回升对进口数量的拉动作用较为明显，根据海关统计（人民币计价），2016 年进口数量指数月均上升 3.7%，第四季度月均上升 4.4%，体现了国内经济逐步企稳的作用。同时，受能源等国际大宗商品价格变动的影响，2016 年 8—12 月进口价格指数月均上升 2.7%，改变了前 7 个月月均下跌 7% 的局面。此外，2016 年，出口数量月均上升 2.7%，出口价格月均下降 2.2%。

货物贸易跨境收付顺差扩大，外币净流入明显增加。 2016 年，我国货物贸易跨境收入较上年下降 9%，跨境支付下降 13%，收付顺差 2 636 亿美元，增长 25%。其中，跨境外汇收付顺差 2 579 亿美元，占总顺差的 98%，2015 年跨境外汇收付顺差 364 亿美元；跨境人民币收付顺差为 57 亿美元，占总顺差的 2%，2015 年跨境人民

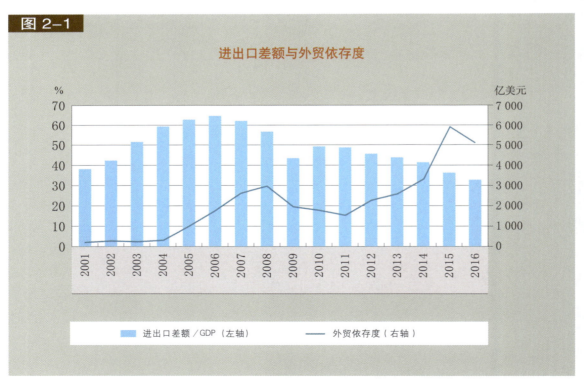

图 2-1

进出口差额与外贸依存度

数据来源：海关总署、国家统计局。

图 2-2

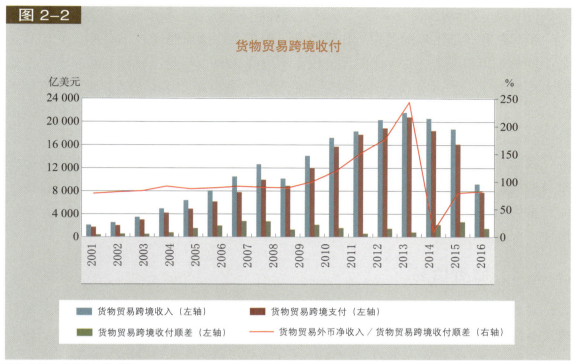

货物贸易跨境收付

数据来源：国家外汇管理局。

图 2-3

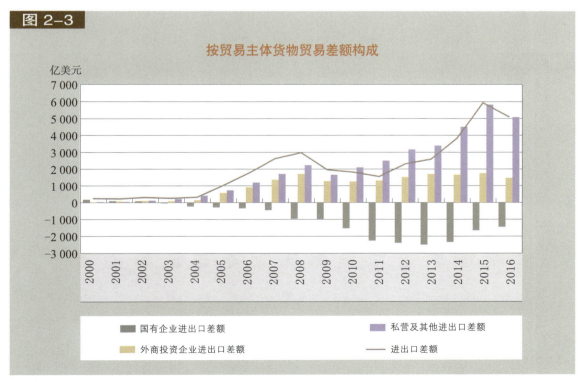

按贸易主体货物贸易差额构成

数据来源：海关总署。

币收付顺差 1 753 亿美元。

私营企业在进出口顺差中的比重上升，外资企业比重略降。2016 年，我国私营企业贸易进出口顺差 4 968 亿美元，较上年下降 12%，相当于总顺差的 97%，占比较上年增加了 3 个百分点；外商投资企业货物进出口顺差 1 465 亿美元，较上年下降 16%，占总顺差的 29%，占比较上年略降 1 个百分点。此外，国有企业货物进出口逆差 1 452 亿美元，较上年下降 12%（见图 2-3）。

我国出口商品在主要发达经济体的份额相对稳定。2016 年，美国进口商品中来自中国的比重为 21%，较上年比重略降 0.4 个百分点；欧盟进口商品中来自中国的比重为 20%，与 2015 年比重基本持平；日本进口商品中来自中国的比重为 26%，增加 1 个百分点。

（二）服务贸易

服务贸易规模保持增长，高附加值服务贸易增速较快。2016 年，我国服务贸易收支总额 6 610 亿美元，较上年增长 1%。同期货物贸易总额为 34 850 亿美元，较上年下降 6%。2016 年服务贸易与货物贸易总额的比例为 19%，较上年增加 1 个百分点（见图 2-5）。服务贸易中，高附加值的服务贸易表现仍优于传统服务贸易。2016 年，加工服务和运输等传统服务贸易收支总额分别以 9% 和 8% 的速度萎缩，而电信、计算机和信息服务以及娱乐、知识产权使用费等高附加值服务贸易收支总额均增长 6% 以上，我国服务贸易结构在相关政策的推动支持下不断优化升级。

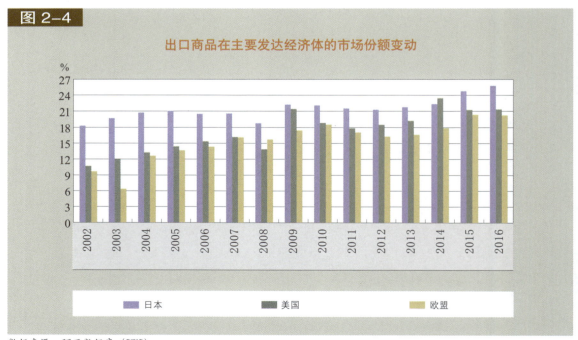

图 2-4　出口商品在主要发达经济体的市场份额变动

数据来源：环亚数据库（CEIC）。

图 2-5

货物贸易和服务贸易收支总额比较

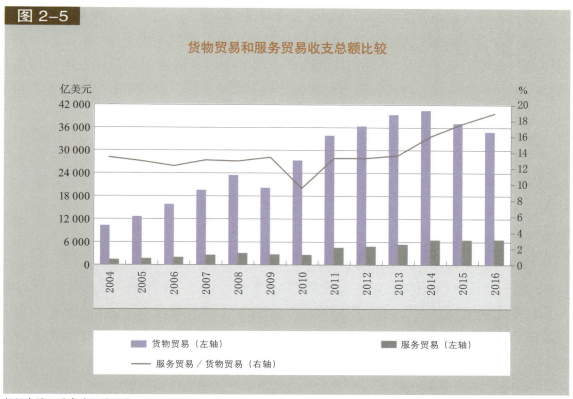

数据来源：国家外汇管理局。

图 2-6

服务贸易收支情况

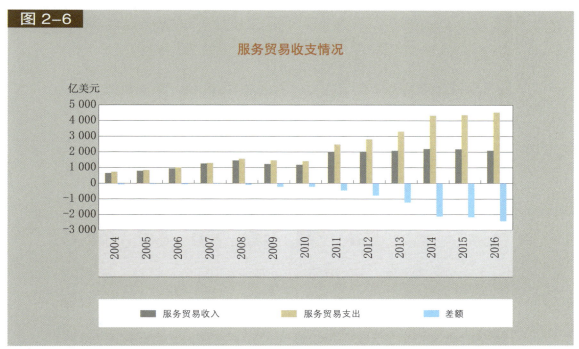

数据来源：国家外汇管理局。

服务贸易收入有所下降。2016 年，服务贸易收入 2 084 亿美元，较上年下降 4%（见图 2-6）。占服务贸易收入比重较大的项目中，旅行收入小幅下降 1%；受全球贸易不景气影响，运输、加工服务及其他商业服务（包括研发成果转让及委托研发，法律、会计、广告等专业和管理咨询服务，技术服务，以及经营性租赁服务等项目）收入分别下降 12%、9% 和 1%。

服务贸易支出小幅增长。2016 年，服务贸易支出 4 526 亿美元，较上年增长 4%。在服务贸易支出比重较大的项目中，旅行占比 58%，较上年增长 1 个百分点，旅行支出较上年增长 5%，增速比上年下降 5 个百分点。运输占比 18%，比重较上年下降 2 个百分点，运输支出较上年下降 6%，降幅比上年收窄 5 个百分点。其他商业服务和知识产权支出较上年均增长 9%，而上年均为减少 3%，涨幅显著。

服务贸易逆差延续扩大趋势。2016 年，服务贸易逆差 2 442 亿美元，较上年增长 12%，增速提高 10 个百分点，旅行逆差仍为服务贸易逆差主要来源（见图 2-7）。2016 年旅行逆差 2 167 亿美元，较上年增长 6%，增速较上年放缓 6 个百分点。随着我国经济发展和国民收入提高，更多国人出国旅游、留学，享受全球化及相关政策不断开放带来的便利，同时，我国居民境外旅游、留学等消费在 2009 年至 2013 年经历了一段高速增长期后，随着相关需求的快速释放，旅行项目逆差增速已开始回稳。

逆差国家和地区保持高集中度趋势。2016 年，我国服务贸易前十大伙伴国（地区）依次为中国香港、美国、日本、韩国、英国、德国、加拿大、澳大利亚、新加

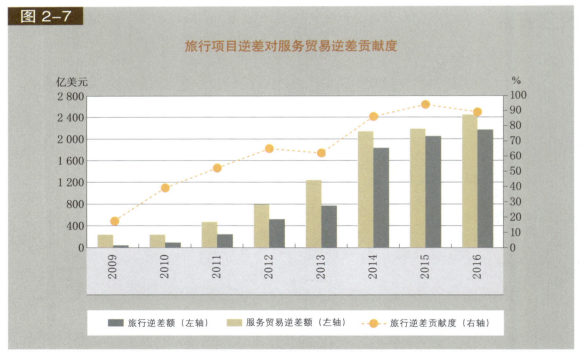

图 2-7 旅行项目逆差对服务贸易逆差贡献度

数据来源：国家外汇管理局。

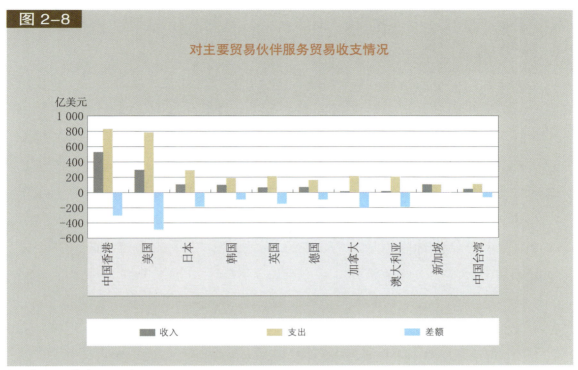

图 2-8

对主要贸易伙伴服务贸易收支情况

亿美元

图例：收入　支出　差额

数据来源：国家外汇管理局。

坡和中国台湾，贸易规模达 4 498 亿美元，占总规模的 68%。其中，除对新加坡为小额顺差外，我国对其余九个主要贸易伙伴国（地区）的服务贸易均呈逆差。对六大贸易伙伴国（地区）逆差均超百亿美元规模（见图 2-8），其中我国对美国服务贸易逆差规模最大，然后依次是中国香港、加拿大、澳大利亚、日本和英国。与上年相比，我国对中国香港、美国、日本、韩国、英国、加拿大、澳大利亚和德国的服务贸易逆差规模有所扩大，对中国台湾的服务贸易逆差规模有所缩小，对新加坡的服务贸易顺差规模略为扩大。

专栏 3

全面采用支付渠道数据　改进国际旅行统计方法

"旅行"是国际收支平衡表中十二大类服务项目之一，在我国国际收支统计中一直占有重要地位。随着统计数据源的不断改善，国家外汇管理局自编制 2016 年全年国际收支平衡表正式数起，全面采用支付渠道数据，协调编制国际旅行收入和旅行支出，并追溯调整 2014 年、2015 年数据。调整后，2016年旅行收入和支出分别从初步统计的 1 182 亿美元和 3 412 亿美元降至 444 亿美元和2 611亿美元，旅行逆差从2 231亿美元略降至2 167亿美元。

一、旅行收支包括了什么

按照国际货币基金组织（IMF）《国际收支和国际投资头寸手册》（第六版）的定义，旅行包括非居民旅行者在旅行地购买自用或馈赠的货物和消费的服务。这里有两个要点，一是非居民旅行者包括因商务和私人目的在外停留一年以下的个人，也包括在境外停留时长不限的学生和就医人员，还包括边境工人、季节性工人和其他短期工人，他（她）们在旅行地的花费全部计入旅行；二是旅行虽在服务项下，但却包含旅行者消费的各类货物和服务，因为旅行项目非常特殊，它以旅行者为统计对象，而无论其消费的是哪类货物或服务（如运输、保险等其他各类服务）都涵盖在旅行项下。基本上，一国居民在境外旅行或就医留学期间的吃穿用度、娱乐消费、学杂费生活费等，均属于旅行的统计范畴。

表 C3-1　旅行项下项目构成一览表

1.A.b.4 旅行
1.A.b.4.1 商务旅行
1.A.b.4.1.1 边境工人、季节性工人和其他短期工人购买的货物和服务
1.A.b.4.1.2 其他
1.A.b.4.2 私人旅行
1.A.b.4.2.1 健康相关旅行
1.A.b.4.2.2 教育相关旅行
1.A.b.4.2.3 其他

资料来源：《国际收支和国际投资头寸手册》（第六版）。

二、如何统计旅行收支

由于旅行收支统计涉及的人员、交易方式、购买的物品或服务非常广泛，实际上无法进行全数统计。国际上通常使用四种方法来测算旅行收支数据，第一种方法是基于旅行支付渠道，最常见的工具是信用卡和借记卡；第二种方法是旅行业企业调查和个人旅行调查，并结合旅客数量调查进行测算；第三种方法是采用伙伴经济体数据；第四种方法是使用数据模型。上述方法可以单独使用，也可以综合运用。

三、我国旅行收支的统计方法

历史上，我国的旅行收支统计曾使用过企业和个人调查数据、伙伴国数据、支付渠道数据及统计估算方法。随着国家外汇管理局于 2014 年新增跨境银行卡统计和 2016 年新增国际旅行现钞花费比例调查,目前,我国国际旅行支付渠道数据已经完备。自编制 2016 年全年国际收支平衡表正式数起,国家外汇管理局全面采用旅行支付渠道数据来编制旅行收入和支出数据。旅行支付渠道涵盖信用卡和借记卡、汇款和现钞,其中,银行卡和汇款数据均为全数统计;现钞数据通过年度个人调查获得的现钞花费比例进行估算。此外,对于"以旅行之名,行投资之实"的交易,也尽可能在可获得的数据范围内进行了还原处理,如境外购房和购买境外投资性保险产品。统计方法调整后,旅行收入和支出数据统计方法协调一致,覆盖完整,从而增强了旅行收支数据的可比性,并且可支持进行双边国家(地区)旅行收支数据测算,丰富了数据维度。

(三)直接投资

直接投资由净流入转为净流出[①]。2016 年,我国国际收支口径的直接投资净流出 466 亿美元(见图 2-9),上年为净流入 681 亿美元。直接投资差额由持续净流入转变为净流出,一方面在于我国企业走出国门、全球资源配置的力度进一步加大,另一方面,外国来华直接投资继续呈现较大净流入,但净流入少增明显。不过,随着我国居民对外投资趋于理性以及外国来华直接投资净流入上升,2016 年第四季度,我国直接投资再度转为净流入。

直接投资资产[②]**增加**。2016 年,我国直接投资资产(主要是我国对外直接投资)净增加 2 172 亿美元,较上年多增 25%(见图 2-10)。继 2014 年首次突破千亿美元后,仅两年时间,我国直接投资资产年净增加额迈上 2 000 亿美元的台阶。我国直接投资资产快速增长是经济发展的必然结果。首先,我国综合实力显著增强推动对外投资快速发展。我国已开始从资本流入阶段转为资本输出阶段,从单纯的商品输出转为商品输出与资本输出并重。其次,企业资产全球优化配置需求也在不断上升。我国企业进入国际市场的意愿明显增强,"一带一路"国家战略的推进和国际产能合作的发展,助推企业加快"走出去"步伐。同时,直接投资资产较快增长也揭示一些值得关注的问题,比如部分领域出现了非理性对外投资的倾向,部分投资出现

---

① 直接投资净流动是指直接投资资产净增加额(资金净流出)与直接投资负债净增加额(资金净流入)之差。当直接投资资产净增加额大于直接投资负债净增加额时,直接投资项目为净流出。反之,则直接投资项目为净流入。

② 直接投资资产以我国对外直接投资为主,但也包括少量境内外商投资企业对境外母公司的反向投资等。

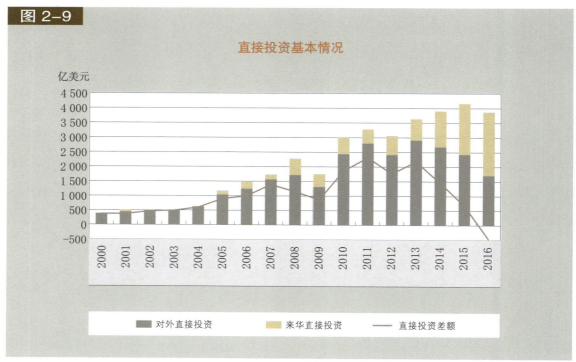

图 2-9

直接投资基本情况

亿美元

对外直接投资　　来华直接投资　　直接投资差额

数据来源：国家外汇管理局。

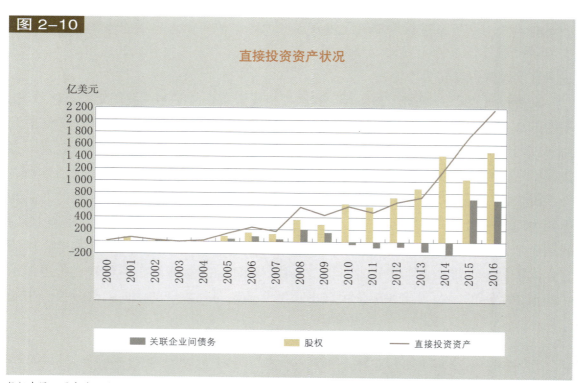

图 2-10

直接投资资产状况

亿美元

关联企业间债务　　股权　　直接投资资产

数据来源：国家外汇管理局。

"母小子大"、"快设快出"等风险隐患。可见，在开展对外投资的同时防范对外投资风险是我国投资者亟待加强的必修课。

从投资形式看，一是股权投资类资产净增加 1 484 亿美元，较上年多增 43%，占新增直接投资资产近七成。直接投资中的股权投资属于长期投资，此类交易较快上升表明境内企业继续注重境外长期投资。二是对境外关联公司贷款等资产净增加 688 亿美元，较上年少增 2%，其中第一季度净增加 297 亿美元，其他三个季度则稳定在百亿美元左右。

分部门看，一是非金融部门的直接投资资产净增加 1 938 亿美元，较上年多增 32%。境内企业对外直接投资目的地排前五位的分别是中国香港、开曼群岛、美国、英属维尔京群岛和新加坡，合计占比 93%，反映我国企业"走出去"高度集中于资金进出管理相对宽松的国家 / 地区。从国内"走出去"的行业看，租赁和商务服务业以及制造业占比近半（见图 2-11）。二是金融部门的直接投资资产净增加 219 亿美元，少增 22%，主要为银行、保险公司和其他金融业的对外直接投资。

直接投资负债[①]继续保持较大净流入。2016 年，直接投资负债净增加 1 706 亿美元，较上年少增 30%。

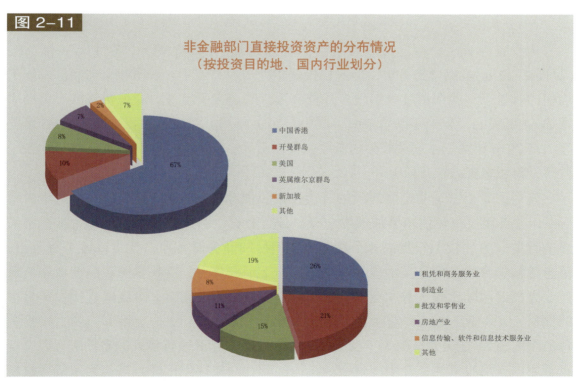

图 2-11

非金融部门直接投资资产的分布情况
（按投资目的地、国内行业划分）

中国香港　开曼群岛　美国　英属维尔京群岛　新加坡　其他

租凭和商务服务业　制造业　批发和零售业　房地产业　信息传输、软件和信息技术服务业　其他

数据来源：国家外汇管理局。

---

① 直接投资负债以吸收来华直接投资为主，但也包括少量境外子公司对境内母公司的反向投资等。

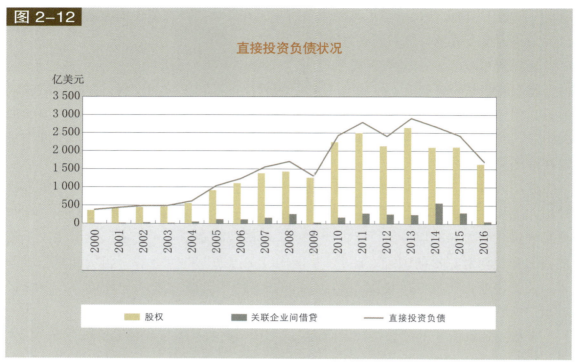

图 2-12

直接投资负债状况

数据来源：国家外汇管理局。

　　从投资形式看，一是股权投资类负债净增加 1 642 亿美元，较上年少增 22%（见图 2-12）。虽然增速下滑，但股权投资仍处于较高水平，表明在全球经济发展不均衡的背景下，我国继续吸引较多外资流入。二是接受境外关联公司贷款等负债净增加 64 亿美元，较上年少增 79%，其中，2016 年第一季度该项目为净还款 35 亿美元。自 2016 年第二季度关联公司贷款恢复净流入，境内主体对外债务去杠杆化告一段落，跨境融资需求开始上升。

　　分部门看，一是非金融部门的直接投资负债净增加 1 625 亿美元，较上年少增 26%，占直接投资负债净增加额的 95%。分行业看，制造业是吸收外来直接投资最多的行业，占比较上年提高 8 个百分点，租赁和商务服务业占比下降 4 个百分点，信息传输、软件及信息技术服务业占比提高 2 个百分点，反映我国在制造业和信息产业方面的国际比较优势和竞争力吸引外资持续流入。同时，对我国直接投资最多的国家 / 地区仍是中国香港，其次是新加坡和中国台湾。二是金融部门的直接投资负债净增加 81 亿美元，较上年少增 66%，这既在于部分银行境外战略投资者因自身经营原因撤出投资，也在于外资金融机构经营利润较往年下降，当年累积留存收益增长有所下滑。

我国企业海外投资的历程和特点

一、企业"走出去"的发展历程

改革开放以来，我国企业"走出去"经历了多个发展阶段，2000 年党的十五届五中全会正式提出"走出去"战略，随后，党中央、国务院陆续提出进一步提高对外开放水平，构建开放型经济新体制等战略，我国对外投资的内涵和外延不断丰富。

第一阶段（1980—1999 年）：改革开放早期以"引进来"为主，对外直接投资（ODI）规模小。**第二阶段（2000—2007 年）**：2000 年后，我国海外投资加快。据商务部统计（下同），2005 年、2006 年 ODI 先后突破 100 亿美元、200 亿美元大关。**第三阶段（2008—2013 年）**：国际金融危机导致海外资产估值相对偏低，我国海外投资进一步加快。2008 年 ODI 首次超过 500 亿美元。2013 年，ODI 突破 1 000 亿美元。**第四阶段（2014 年至今）**：ODI 逐步接近并超过利用外资规模。

二、企业"走出去"的主要特点

起步晚，增长快，潜力大。从流量看，2003—2015 年，我国非金融类 ODI 年均增长 33%。从存量上看，2015 年我国 ODI 存量首次突破万亿美元。2003—2015 年间 ODI 存量的年均增长率达 30%。截至 2014 年末，我国 ODI 存量相当于 GDP 的 7%，与美国 38%、日本 20% 和德国 47% 仍有较大差距。

投资区域亚洲独大，逐步向发达国家拓展。从流量上看，2007 年以来，我国对亚洲直接投资一直保持在 70% 的较高比例。从存量上看，亚洲、欧洲和拉丁美洲分别占 68%、12% 和 8%。

行业转型趋势明显，行业分布趋于分散。采矿业占 ODI 流量从 2003 年的 48% 下降到 2015 年的 8%；租赁和服务业同期从 10% 提高到 25%（见图 C4-1）。2015 年底 ODI 存量中，租赁和服务业占比 37%。

民企、国企并驾齐驱。2006 年末，国有企业占 ODI 存量的 81%，非国有企业只占 19%。2015 年末，国有企业占 50%；非国有企业占 50%，将近平分秋色。

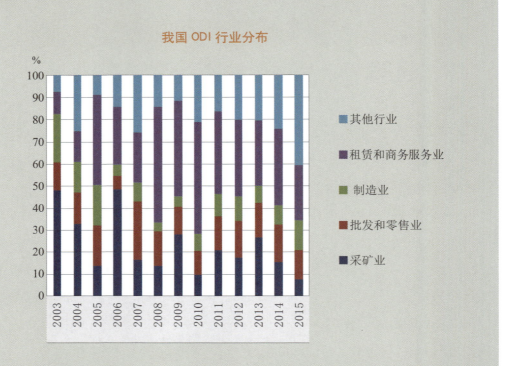

图 C4-1

我国 ODI 行业分布

其他行业
租赁和商务服务业
制造业
批发和零售业
采矿业

数据来源：Wind 资讯数据库。

海外投资与大宗商品价格具有顺周期性。2011—2012 年，大宗商品价格达到历史最高点，同期我国企业能矿海外并购金额也达到当年我国企业海外并购总额的 64%。2016 年以来，随着大宗商品价格下降，能矿海外并购交易量下降至仅占海外并购总额的 2%。

控股收购主导。2016 年第一季度，控股收购金额 1 008 亿美元，占比 96%；前十大并购交易中有九个项目为全额收购。从交易笔数看，在 199 笔交易中，控股收购 137 笔，占比 77%。

总的来看，当前我国对外直接投资较快增长体现了综合国力的提升、对外开放程度的提高以及"一带一路"倡议和国际产能合作等措施的稳步推进，有益于促进经济增长，实现互利共赢、共同发展。但 2016 年以来我国企业对外直接投资中也出现了一些不够理性的倾向和异常情况，需要积极引导，使其更加健康、有序。我国关于对外直接投资的方针政策和管理原则是明确的。鼓励企业参与国际经济竞争与合作，促进国内经济转型升级，深化我国与世界各国的互利合作；遵循"企业主体、市场原则、国际惯例、政府引导"的原则，支持国内有能力、有条件的企业开展真实合规的对外投资活动。

（四）证券投资

证券投资净流出略有收窄。2016 年证券投资项下净流出 622 亿美元，较上年下降 6%（见图 2-13）。其中，第一季度证券投资大幅流出，第二季度由净流出转为净流入，第三季度重回净流出，第四季度净流出扩大。从交易项目看，股权投资净流出减少而债券投资净流出增加。2016 年股权投资净流出 196 亿美元，下降 21%；债券投资净流出 426 亿美元，增长 2%。

对外证券投资净流出继续增长。2016 年，我国对外证券投资净流出 1 034 亿美元，较上年增长 41%。其中，股权投资净流出 385 亿美元，下降 3%；债券投资净流出 649 亿美元，增长 93%。

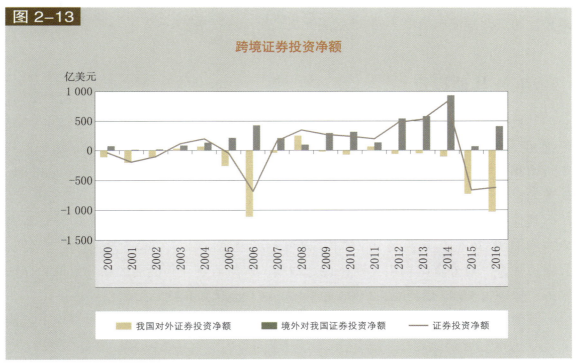

图 2-13

跨境证券投资净额

亿美元

（图例）我国对外证券投资净额　　境外对我国证券投资净额　　证券投资净额

注：我国对外证券投资正值表示减持对外股权或债券，负值表示增持对外股权或债券；境外对我国证券投资正值表示增加对国内股权或债权投资，负值表示减少对国内股权或债券投资。

数据来源：国家外汇管理局。

从对外证券投资的渠道看，一是金融机构对外债务证券投资大幅攀升，2016年净流出规模为482亿美元，增长51%。二是资本市场开放带来股权投资双向流动加大，"港股通"投资净流出从上年的133亿美元升至273亿美元，增长105%。三是合格境内机构投资者（QDII及RQDII）投资净流出缩减，2016年QDII及RQDII投资非居民发行的股票和债券合计57亿美元，较上年减少163亿美元。四是我国居民购买非居民境内发行债券60亿美元，增长4倍。

境外对我国证券投资大增，开放债券市场是主要原因。2016年，境外对我国证券投资净流入412亿美元，较上年增长512%；除第一季度净流出189亿美元外，其他三个季度均为净流入。其中，境外对我国股权投资净流入189亿美元，增长27%；债券投资净流入223亿美元，上年为净流出82亿美元，债券投资由逆转顺是境外对我国证券投资较上年大增的主要原因。2016年，我国进一步放开境外投资者投资银行间债券市场，实施合格境外机构投资者外汇管理改革，放宽其投资额度限制，便利资金汇出入等，跨境资金流入渠道持续扩大。

从境外对我国证券投资的主要渠道看，一是境外机构投资境内债券市场370亿美元，较上年增加281亿美元；二是非居民购买我国机构境外发行的股票、债券由上年的357亿美元下降至256亿美元；三是"沪股通"和"深股通"渠道流入资金由上年的30亿美元提高到69亿美元；四是银行承兑远期信用证（附汇票）余额[①]下降导致的资金净流出由上年的85亿美元提高至283亿美元。

（五）其他投资

其他投资净流出下降。2016年，我国其他投资项下净流出（净资产增加）3 035亿美元，较上年下降30%（见图2-14）。其他投资主要子项目净流出均有趋缓，其中货币和存款、贷款、贸易信贷净资产增加分别为333亿美元、1 343亿美元和846亿美元，较上年分别少增81%、37%和22%。

其他投资项下对外资本输出继续增加。2016年，我国其他投资项下对外资本输出净增加3 336亿美元，较上年增长305%。境内主体参与国际经济活动较为活跃，且增速加快。对外资本输出主要体现为贷款、贸易信贷、其他资产以及货币和存款增加，分别为1 147亿美元、1 008亿美元、743亿美元和435亿美元。

其他投资项下对外负债由净流出转为净流入。2016年，我国其他投资项下负债

---

① 按照《国际收支和国际投资头寸手册》（第六版）原则，附带汇票的承兑远期信用证从"其他投资/贷款"转入"证券投资/债务证券"项下统计。

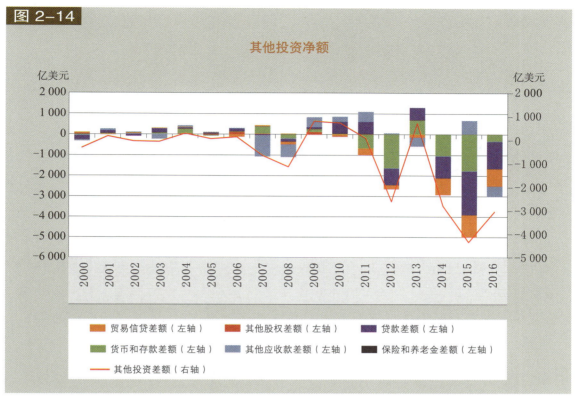

图 2-14

其他投资净额

数据来源：国家外汇管理局。

净流入（即我国对外负债净增加）301 亿美元，而上年为净流出 3 515 亿美元。一方面，境外贷款资金净流出 196 亿美元，较上年下降 88%，自 2016 年第二季度以来，随着前期外债去杠杆化告一段落，全口径跨境融资宏观审慎管理等便利企业跨境融资的政策落地，我国企业利用外债开始回升，2016 年后三个季度境外贷款资金均为净流入。另一方面，我国吸收的货币和存款类资金净流入 102 亿美元，上年为净流出 1 226 亿美元，其中非居民人民币存款下降 477 亿美元，较上年少降 51%。另外，贸易信贷负债增加 162 亿美元（即贸易项下应付和预收增长），上年为减少 623 亿美元。其他负债增加 239 亿美元，主要是我国央行对国际货币基金组织认缴份额形成其在央行的债权增加。

专栏 5

不同类型企业贸易信贷工具运用存在差异

2016 年 8 月，新版《贸易信贷调查制度》正式实施，样本企业首次报送 7 月数据。与旧制度相比，调查企业由分层抽样改为规模以上企业调查，统计口径调整为依照企业会计账，填报全口径贸易应收应付，不再按照权责区分银行融资或者企业信贷[①]。从样本企业情况看，不同类型的样本企业对贸易信贷工具的运用存在差异。

制造业和批发零售业位居贸易信贷规模前两位，个别行业贸易信贷具有明显特征。制造业和批发零售业企业在应收、应付、预收、预付中的合计占比分别为 95%、93%、84% 和 66%，是贸易信贷最主要的运用者，其中又以电子设备制造业规模最大（应收和应付占比均超过 50%）。运输设备制造业和航空运输业较为特殊，分别在出口预收和进口预付中的占比（23% 和 32%）远高于其在出口和进口中占比（2% 和 1%）。

外商投资企业利用贸易信贷融通资金，规避汇率风险甚至主动开展财务运作获取收益的意识高于内资企业。一是出口应收和进口预付中分别有 57% 和 43% 来自外资企业，低于外资企业在出口和进口中的占比（60% 和 52%），但从月度数据看，外资企业在出口应收中的比例由 7 月的 52% 升至 11 月的 57%，是出口应收规模增长的主要来源。二是进口应付中 62% 来自外资企业，高于外资企业在进口中的占比 10 个百分点。外资企业在汇率及利率等环境变化下，利用跨境资金调度的天然优势开展财务运作，对贸易信贷资产工具尤其是应收的运用明显增加，通过资金滞留境外获取收益。

大型企业运用贸易信贷的能力较强，预收预付的集中度高于应收应付。一是前 10 家和前 100 家样本企业的应收、预收、应付和预付占全部样本企业的比例均远高于其出口和进口规模占比。二是出口预收和进口预付集中度更高，前 100 家样本企业占比高达 75% 和 96%（对应出口和进口占比仅为 6% 和 12%）。三是出口应收和进口应付排名前 100 家的样本企业中分别有 61 家和 46 家来自电子设备制造业。

[①] 专栏 5 中数据根据 2016 年 7—11 月贸易信贷调查结果得出，贸易信贷数据为样本企业报送的全口径贸易信贷数据，即包含企业信用的贸易信贷和银行贸易融资。

　　出口应收和进口应付中近六成为对关联企业的贸易信贷，大型企业、外资企业、制造业企业与关联企业的应收应付往来较多。一是出口应收和进口应付中分别有57%和55%来自关联企业，而出口预收和进口预付中关联企业占比仅为10%和16%，关联企业之间通过应收应付来融通资金较为常见。二是大型企业关联交易情况比较突出，出口应收和进口应付排名前10家企业与关联企业之间的余额占比分别为81%和82%。三是外资企业的应收、应付款较多从境外母公司或关联企业处获得，占比分别为79%和68%。四是制造业企业与关联企业的应收应付往来较多，尤其是电子设备制造业对关联企业的应收、应付占全部应收、应付的比例分别达到81%和66%。

三、国际投资头寸状况

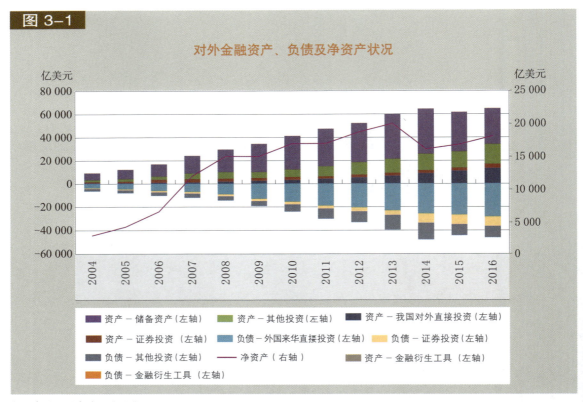

图 3-1

对外金融资产、负债及净资产状况

图例：
- 资产－储备资产（左轴）
- 资产－其他投资（左轴）
- 资产－我国对外直接投资（左轴）
- 资产－证券投资（左轴）
- 负债－外国来华直接投资（左轴）
- 负债－证券投资（左轴）
- 负债－其他投资（左轴）
- 净资产（右轴）
- 资产－金融衍生工具（左轴）
- 负债－金融衍生工具（左轴）

数据来源：国家外汇管理局。

对外金融资产和负债[①] **均有所回升，对外净资产增长。** 2016 年末，我国对外金融资产 64 666 亿美元，对外负债 46 660 亿美元，较上年末分别增长 5% 和 4%；对外净资产 18 005 亿美元，较上年末增加 1 277 亿美元，增长 8%（见图 3-1）。

对外资产中民间部门持有占比首次过半。 2016 年末，我国对外金融资产中，直接投资资产 13 172 亿美元，较上年末增长 20%，占资产总额的比重升至历史最高值 20%，较上年末增加约 3 个百分点；证券投资资产 3 651 亿美元，较上年末增长 40%，占比为 6%，较上年末增加 1 个百分点；存贷款等其他投资资产 16 811 亿美元，较上年末增长 21%，占比为 26%，较上年末增加 3 个百分点；国际储备资产余额为 30 978 亿美元，较上年末减少 9%，其中外汇储备余额 30 105 亿美元，较上年末减少 10%。储备资产占我国对外金融资产总额的 48%，继续占据对外资产首位，但比重较上年末减少 7 个百分点，为 2004 年公布国际投资头寸数据以来的最低比重水平（见图 3-2）。

我国对外负债增长主要是由于来华直接投资保持增长和来华其他投资回升。

① 对外金融资产和负债包括直接投资、证券投资及存贷款等其他投资。之所以对外直接投资属于金融资产范畴，是因为境内投资者持有的是境外被投资企业的股权，这与证券投资中的股权投资无本质区别，只是直接投资通常持股比例较高，意在影响或控制企业的生产经营活动。反之，外来直接投资则属于对外金融负债范畴，也是境外投资者对外商投资企业的权益。

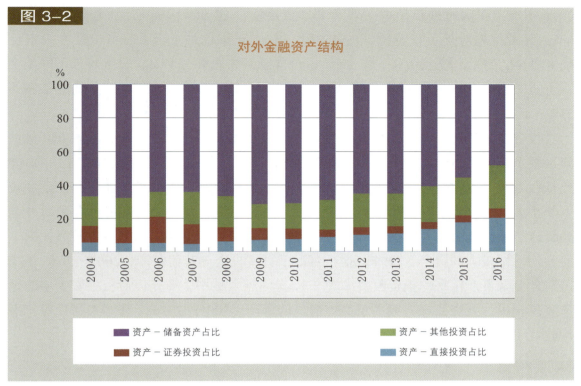

图 3-2

对外金融资产结构

图例：
- 资产－储备资产占比
- 资产－证券投资占比
- 资产－其他投资占比
- 资产－直接投资占比

数据来源：国家外汇管理局。

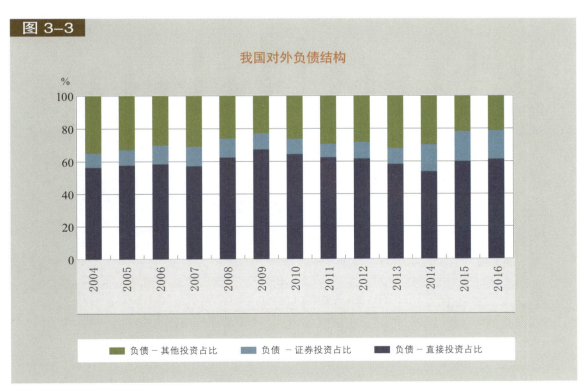

图 3-3

我国对外负债结构

图例：
- 负债－其他投资占比
- 负债－证券投资占比
- 负债－直接投资占比

数据来源：国家外汇管理局。

2016 年末，我国对外负债中，外国来华直接投资 28 659 亿美元①，较上年末增长 6%，继续位列对外负债首位，占比 61%，较上年末增加 1 个百分点；证券投资负债 8 086 亿美元，较上年末下降 1%，占负债总额的比重为 17%，较上年末下降 1 个百分点；存贷款等其他投资负债 9 849 亿美元，较上年末增长 2%，占负债总额的 21%，较上年末略降 0.4 个百分点（见图 3-3）。

投资收益逆差收窄。2016 年，我国国际收支平衡表中投资收益为逆差 650 亿美元，较上年减少 6%。其中，我国对外投资收益收入 1 984 亿美元，增长 5%；对外负债收益支出 2 634 亿美元，增长 2%；二者收益率差异为 -2.6 个百分点，差额较上年扩大 0.1 个百分点（见图 3-4）。长期来看，投资收益差额为负是由我国对外金融资产负债结构决定的。2016 年末我国对外金融资产中储备资产仍占比较高，因主要为流动性较强的资产，投资回报相对低于直接投资等其他资产，2005—2016 年我国对外金融资产年平均投资收益率为 3.3%；对外负债中主要是以股权投资为主的来华直接投资，投资回报一般高于其他形式的资产，2005—2016 年外国来华投资年平均收益率为 6.4%。

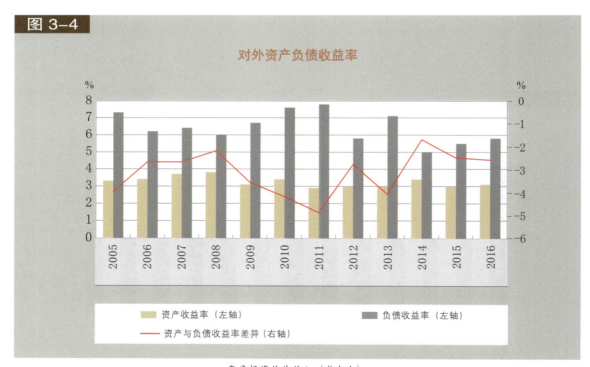

注：1. 资产（或负债）收益率 = 年度投资收益收入（或支出） / [（上年末 + 本年末对外资产（或负债）存量）/2]

　　2. 资产负债收益率差异 = 资产收益率 - 负债收益率
数据来源：国家外汇管理局。

_____

① 外国来华直接投资存量包括我国非金融部门和金融部门吸收来华直接投资存量，以及境内外母子公司间贷款和其他债务性往来，并反映了价值重估因素影响。该口径与商务部统计的累计吸收外商直接投资不同，后者是历年外商直接投资股本投资流量的累加。

表 3-1　2016 年末中国国际投资头寸表　　　　　　　　　　　　　单位：亿美元

项目	行次	2016 年末
净头寸①	1	18 005
资产	2	64 666
1 直接投资	3	13 172
1.1 股权	4	10 650
1.2 关联企业债务	5	2 522
2 证券投资	6	3 651
2.1 股权	7	2 149
2.2 债券	8	1 502
3 金融衍生工具	9	52
4 其他投资	10	16 811
4.1 其他股权	11	1
4.2 货币和存款	12	3 816
4.3 贷款	13	5 622
4.4 保险和养老金	14	123
4.5 贸易信贷	15	6 145
4.6 其他	16	1 105
5 储备资产	17	30 978
5.1 货币黄金	18	679
5.2 特别提款权	19	97
5.3 在国际货币基金组织的储备头寸	20	96
5.4 外汇储备	21	30 105
5.5 其他储备资产	22	2
负债	23	46 660
1 直接投资	24	28 659
1.1 股权	25	26 543
1.2 关联企业债务	26	2 117
2 证券投资	27	8 086
2.1 股权	28	5 927
2.2 债券	29	2 159
3 金融衍生工具	30	66
4 其他投资	31	9 849
4.1 其他股权	32	0
4.2 货币和存款	33	3 156
4.3 贷款	34	3 236
4.4 保险和养老金	35	88
4.5 贸易信贷	36	2 883
4.6 其他	37	391
4.7 特别提款权	38	94

数据来源：国家外汇管理局。

① 净头寸是指资产减负债，"＋"表示净资产，"—"表示净负债。本表记数采用四舍五入原则。

专栏6

我国银行业对外资产负债结构分析

2016 年末，我国银行业对外资产和对外负债规模较上年末均增长，对外净负债下降。其中，对外资产 8 776 亿美元[①]，增长 19%，占我国对外金融资产存量[②] 的 14%；对外负债 9 645 亿美元，增长 2%，占我国对外负债存量的 21%；对外净负债 869 亿美元，下降 59%。

对外金融资产中存贷款占八成，债券资产占比低但增速最高，对境外子行增资带来股权等其他投资增加。我国银行业对境外发放贷款和在境外存款 6 705 亿美元，较上年末增长 16%，占比 76%，主要是对境外发放的贷款；投资境外债券 952 亿美元，增长 50%，占比 11%，主要是增持了美国和中国香港市场发行的债券；对外股权和金融衍生品等其他投资资产 1 119 亿美元，增长 12%，占比 13%，主要是增加了对境外子行的股权投资。

对外负债中存贷款占比过半，债券负债有所下降，银行赴境外上市等带来股权等其他负债增加。我国银行业吸收境外存款和接受境外贷款 5 011 亿美元，较上年末增长 3%，占比 52%，其中主要是从境外关联银行获得的贷款；对外债券负债 1 169 亿美元，下降 16%，占比 12%，主要是与贸易有关的承兑远期信用证负债到期偿还所致；股权和金融衍生品等其他投资负债 3 464 亿美元，增长 8%，占比 36%，主要是境内银行如邮政储蓄银行境外上市，带来对外股权类负债增加（见图 C6-1）。

从币种结构来看，对外外币为净资产，人民币为净负债。2016 年末，银行业对外美元资产 5 986 亿美元，较上年末增长 11%，占比 68%，主要来自增加发放美元贷款和增持美元债券；人民币资产 1 176 亿美元，较上年末增长 1 倍，占比 13%，主要来自增加发放境外人民币贷款；其他外币资产 1 614 亿美元，占比 19%。我国银行业对外美元负债 3 431 亿美元，较上年末增长 47%，占比 36%；人民币负债 3 029 亿美元，较上年末减少 31%，占比 31%；其他外币负债 3 184 亿美元，占比 33%。从资产负债净额看，我国对外人民币净负债

[①] 本文所用数据来自国家外汇管理局《对外金融资产负债及交易统计制度》采集的数据。我国已于 2015 年底参加国际清算银行的国际银行业统计，并按照其要求分季度报送我国银行业的对外资产负债情况，本文基于 2016 年 12 月末报送数据进行分析。

[②] 对外资产存量规模含储备资产，若扣除储备资产，银行业对外资产占比为 26%。

图 C6-1

银行业对外金融资产结构

亿美元

图例：
- 资产－其他资产
- 资产－债券
- 资产－存款和贷款
- 负债－其他负债
- 负债－债券
- 负债－存款和贷款

数据来源：国家外汇管理局。

图 C6-2

银行业对外金融资产和负债币种结构

单位：亿美元

左图数值：2 671、3 029、8、36、132、337、3 431

右图数值：636、83、322、1 139、1 176、5 986

左图图例：
- 瑞士法郎
- 人民币
- 英镑
- 欧元
- 美元
- 日元
- 其他外币

右图图例：
- 人民币
- 欧元
- 英镑
- 瑞士法郎
- 其他外币
- 日元
- 美元

数据来源：国家外汇管理局。

1 853 亿美元，较上年末减少 51%；外币净资产 984 亿美元，减少 42%。

    从国家和地区分布来看，对外资产和负债的对手方主要为发达国家（地区）及离岸中心。我国银行业对外金融资产投向前三位国家（地区）依次是：对中国香港资产 2 244 亿美元，对美国 1 131 亿美元，对新加坡 345 亿美元，分别占总资产的 26%、13% 和 4%。我国银行业对外负债来源前三位国家（地区）依次是：对中国香港负债 5 242 亿美元，对中国台湾负债 598 亿美元，对日本负债 368 亿美元，分别占 54%、6% 和 4%。

表 C6-1　2016 年我国银行业对外资产负债结构表　　　　　　　　　　　　　　　　单位：亿美元，%

		资　产		负　债		净资产
		金　额	占　比	金　额	占　比	金　额
按工具类型分	存贷款	6 705	76	5 011	52	1 694
	债券	952	11	1 169	12	−218
	其他	1 119	13	3 464	36	−2 345
按币种分	人民币	1 176	13	3 029	31	−1 853
	美元	5 986	68	3 431	36	2 555
	欧元	322	4	337	3	−15
	日元	83	1	132	1	−49
	英镑	63	1	36	0.4	27
	其他	1 145	13	2 680	28	−1 534
合计		8 776	100	9 645	100	−869

数据来源：国家外汇管理局。

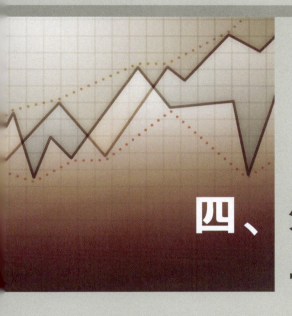

四、外汇市场运行与人民币汇率

（一）人民币汇率走势

人民币对主要货币有升有贬。2016 年末，人民币对美元汇率中间价为 6.9370 元 / 美元，较 2015 年末贬值 6.4%，境内市场（CNY）和境外市场（CNH）即期交易价累计分别贬值 6.5% 和 5.8%（见图 4-1），境内外市场日均价差 134 个基点（见图 4-2），低于 2015 年全年日均价差（213 个基点）。

2016 年末，人民币对欧元、日元、英镑、澳元、加元汇率中间价分别为 7.3068 元 / 欧元、5.9591 元 /100 日元、8.5094 元 / 英镑、5.0157 元 / 澳元、5.1406 元 / 加元，分别较上年末贬值 2.9%、贬值 9.6%、升值 13%、贬值 5.7% 和贬值 8.9%。

人民币对一篮子货币小幅贬值。根据中国外汇交易中心的数据，2016 年末 CFETS 人民币汇率指数、参考 BIS 货币篮子和 SDR 货币篮子的人民币汇率指数分别为 94.83、96.24 和 95.50，较上年末分别贬值 6.1%、5.4% 和 3.4%。

根据国际清算银行（BIS）的数据，2016 年人民币名义有效汇率累计贬值 5.8%，扣除通货膨胀因素的实际有效汇率累计贬值 5.7%（见图 4-3）；2005 年人民币汇率形成机制改革以来，人民币名义和实际有效汇率累计分别升值 37.3% 和 47.1%。

人民币汇率预期基本稳定。2016 年末，境内外市场人民币对美元汇率 1 年期历史波动率分别为 2.7% 和 3.4%，较上年末分别下降 12.3% 和 21.4%；期权市场隐含

图 4-1

境内外人民币对美元即期汇率

数据来源：中国外汇交易中心、路透数据库。

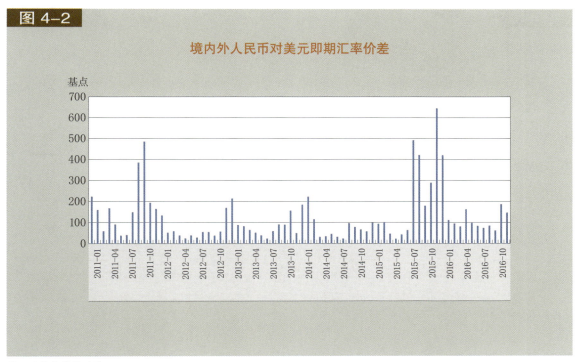

图 4-2

境内外人民币对美元即期汇率价差

注：日均价差绝对值。
数据来源：中国外汇交易中心，路透数据库。

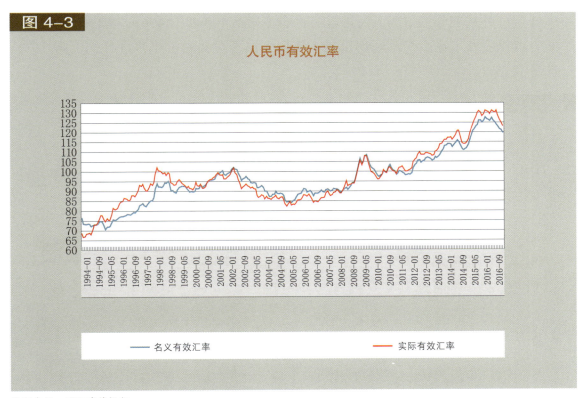

图 4-3

人民币有效汇率

— 名义有效汇率   — 实际有效汇率

数据来源：国际清算银行。

图 4-4

境内外市场人民币对美元汇率 1 年期波动率

期权隐含被动率

历史波动率

数据来源：彭博资讯。

波动率分别为 5.2% 和 8.1%，较上年末分别增长 2.9% 和 8.7%（见图 4-4），人民币汇率在双向波动中保持基本稳定。

远期外汇市场人民币走弱。受本外币利差、外汇供求、市场预期等因素影响，2016 年境内外远期外汇市场人民币震荡走弱（见图 4-5 和图 4-6），境内可交割、境外可交割和境外无本金交割远期市场 1 年期人民币对美元汇率累计分别下跌 5.7%、7.3% 和 7.3%。

图 4-5

境内外远期市场 1 年期人民币对美元汇率

数据来源：中国外汇交易中心、路透数据库。

图 4-6

境内人民币与美元利差（6 个月期限）

利差 1（人民币 Shibor－境内美元拆借）　　利差 2（外汇掉期隐含）
利差 2－利差 1

数据来源：中国外汇交易中心、路透数据库。

（二）外汇市场交易

2016 年，人民币外汇市场累计成交 20 万亿美元（日均 832 亿美元），较上年增长 14%（见图 4-7）。其中，银行对客户市场和银行间外汇市场分别成交 3 万亿美元和 17 万亿美元[①]；即期和衍生产品分别成交 9 万亿美元和 11 万亿美元（见表 4-1），衍生产品在外汇市场交易总量中的比重升至历史新高的 56%，交易产品构成进一步接近全球外汇市场状况（见图 4-8）。

即期外汇交易增长。 2016 年，即期市场累计成交 9 万亿美元，较上年增长 7%。在市场分布上，银行对客户即期结售汇（含银行自身，不含远期履约）累计 2.9 万亿美元，较上年下降 14%；银行间即期外汇市场累计成交 6 万亿美元，较上年增长 22%，其中美元交易份额为 97%。

远期外汇交易下降。 2016 年，远期市场累计成交 3 783 亿美元，较上年下降 24%。在市场分布上，银行对客户远期结售汇累计签约 2 254 亿美元，其中结汇和售汇分别为 703 亿美元和 1 551 亿美元，较上年分别下降 51%、47% 和 52%（见图 4-9），6 个月以内的短期交易占 59%，较上年下降 11.4 个百分点；银行间远期外汇

---

① 银行对客户市场采用客户买卖外汇总额，银行间外汇市场采用单边交易量，以下同。

图 4-7

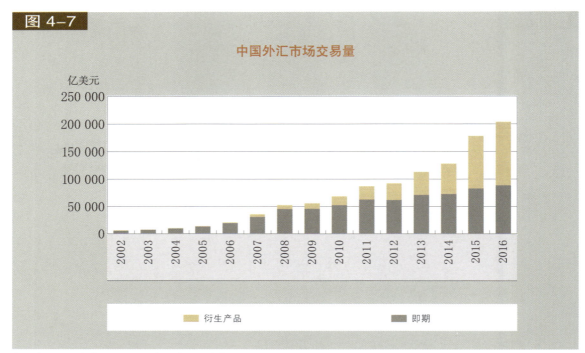

中国外汇市场交易量

数据来源：国家外汇管理局、中国外汇交易中心。

图 4-8

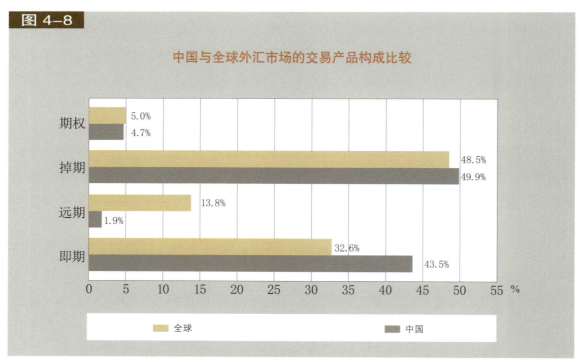

中国与全球外汇市场的交易产品构成比较

注：中国为 2016 年数据，全球为国际清算银行 2016 年 4 月调查数据。
数据来源：国家外汇管理局、中国外汇交易中心、国际清算银行。

市场累计成交 1 529 亿美元，较上年增长 3.1 倍。

掉期交易增长。2016 年，外汇和货币掉期市场累计成交 10 万亿美元，较上年增长 18%。在市场分布上，银行对客户外汇和货币掉期累计签约 1 068 亿美元，较上年下降 56%，其中近端结汇 / 远端购汇和近端购汇 / 远端结汇的交易量分别为 736 亿美元和 331 亿美元，较上年分别增长 2.5 倍和下降 85%，主要反映了远期美元升水点数大幅收窄对企业交易行为的影响；银行间外汇和货币掉期市场累计成交 10 万亿美元，较上年增长 20%。

外汇期权交易增长。2016 年，期权市场累计成交 9 550 亿美元，较上年增长 1.4 倍，显示在人民币汇率双向浮动环境下，期权交易对于管理汇率风险的灵活性和吸引力进一步突出。在市场分布上，银行对客户期权市场累计成交 2 079 亿美元，较上年增长 79%；银行间外汇期权市场累计成交 7 471 亿美元，较上年增长 1.6 倍。

外汇市场参与者结构基本稳定。银行自营交易延续主导地位（见图 4–10），2016 年银行间交易占整个外汇市场的比重从 2015 年的 75.4% 提高至 82%；非金融客户交易的比重从 23% 下降至 17%，非银行金融机构交易的市场份额小幅下降 0.7 个百分点至 0.8%。

图 4-9

银行对客户远期结售汇交易量

亿美元

结汇　售汇　差额　总额

数据来源：国家外汇管理局。

图 4-10

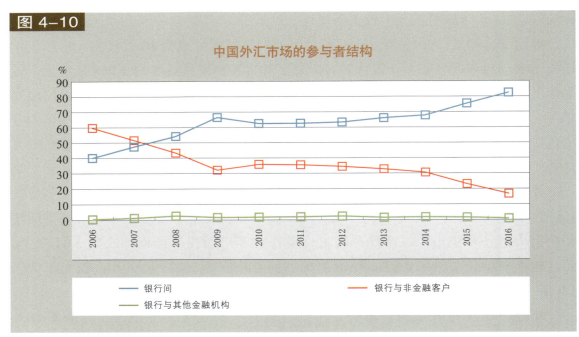

中国外汇市场的参与者结构

银行间
银行与其他金融机构
银行与非金融客户

数据来源：国家外汇管理局、中国外汇交易中心。

表 4-1 2016 年人民币外汇市场交易概况

交易品种	交易量（亿美元）
即期	88 354
银行对客户市场	29 085
银行间外汇市场	59 269
远期	3 783
银行对客户市场	2 254
其中：3 个月（含）以下	895
3 个月至 1 年（含）	1 154
1 年以上	205
银行间外汇市场	1 529
其中：3 个月（含）以下	1 195
3 个月至 1 年（含）	305
1 年以上	28
外汇和货币掉期	101 297
银行对客户市场	1 068
银行间外汇市场	100 229
其中：3 个月（含）以下	88 520
3 个月至 1 年（含）	11 592
1 年以上	117
期权	9 550
银行对客户市场	2 079
其中：买入期权	1 021

续表

交易品种	交易量（亿美元）
卖出期权	1 058
其中：3 个月（含）以下	668
3 个月至 1 年（含）	1 196
1 年以上	215
银行间外汇市场	7 471
其中：3 个月（含）以下	6 998
3 个月至 1 年（含）	468
1 年以上	4
合计	202 984
银行对客户市场	34 486
银行间外汇市场	168 498
其中：即期	88 354
远期	3 783
外汇和货币掉期	101 297
期权	9 550

注：数据均为单边交易额，采用四舍五入原则。
数据来源：国家外汇管理局、中国外汇交易中心。

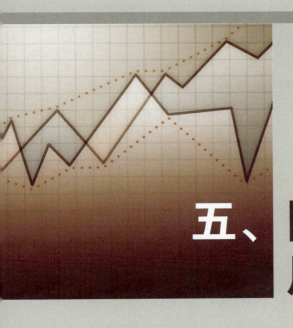

五、国际收支形势展望

2017 年，我国国际收支仍将呈现"经常账户顺差、资本和金融账户（不含储备资产，下同）逆差"的格局，跨境资本流动继续向着均衡状态收敛。

经常账户顺差将继续保持在合理区间。首先，货物贸易顺差仍会维持一定规模。从出口看，尽管贸易摩擦对我国出口形成一些潜在威胁，但 2017 年全球经济总体企稳仍是我国外需稳定的基本保障。根据国际货币基金组织最新预测，2017 年全球经济增长 3.4%，较 2016 年增速提升 0.3 个百分点，其中发达经济体、新兴市场和发展中经济体增速分别回升 0.3 个和 0.4 个百分点。同时，随着"一带一路"等相关合作稳步推进，区域内国家出口都会受益。从进口看，我国经济基本面总体较好，国际大宗商品价格将有所回升，进口规模有望趋向基本稳定。其次，服务贸易逆差增速将逐步趋稳。我国服务贸易逆差主要来自旅行项目，随着近两年居民境外旅游、留学等消费需求快速释放，旅行项目逆差增速已开始回稳；我国企业服务贸易收入和支出结构正在逐步调整，旅行之外的服务贸易逆差已明显收窄。此外，近几年我国对外直接投资等私人部门投资增多，我国境外投资整体收益有望继续增长。预计 2017 年经常账户顺差与 GDP 之比仍将处于均衡合理水平。

资本和金融账户逆差有望收窄。一方面，国际环境不稳定、不确定因素仍较多，可能造成市场情绪多变，引起我国跨境资金流动阶段性波动。美国特朗普政府政策调整、英国后续脱欧谈判路径、欧洲主要国家大选结果等政治经济事件尚不明朗，经济全球化进程也可能遭受挑战；美联储货币政策干扰因素增多，市场对其加息节奏的预期复杂多变；此外，地缘政治冲突和国际恐怖主义多发极易触发局部紧张形势。另一方面，一些有利于跨境资本流出入趋向均衡的因素仍会发挥积极作用。一是近期国内经济有所回稳，相关风险总体可控，国家出台扩大对外开放积极利用外资的政策措施，外商投资环境继续优化，有利于推动长期资本流入。二是近几年随着我国企业综合实力和全球资源配置需求的提升，我国对外直接投资迎来高速增长期，在经历了短期的快速增长后，企业的投资风险意识逐步增强，对外投资将会更加理性和平稳。三是在扩大金融市场对外开放政策方面，我国实施了全口径跨境融资宏观审慎管理、推动银行间债券市场进一步开放、深化 QFII 和 RQFII 外汇管理改革等政策，政策效果已开始显现，未来将继续吸引跨境资金持续流入。四是随着人民币汇率市场化形成机制改革稳步推进，人民币汇率弹性将进一步增强，有利于促进我国跨境资本流动呈现有进有出、双向波动的格局。

2017 年，外汇管理部门将按照稳中求进的工作总基调，兼顾便利化和防风险。一方面，继续深化外汇管理改革，推进汇率市场化改革，扩大金融市场对外开放，促进贸易投资便利化，服务实体经济发展。另一方面，加强真实性合规性审核，严厉打击外汇领域违规违法活动，维护良性的外汇市场秩序，加强事中事后管理，完善宏观审慎跨境资本流动管理框架，防范跨境资本流动风险，切实促进外汇市场健康发展。

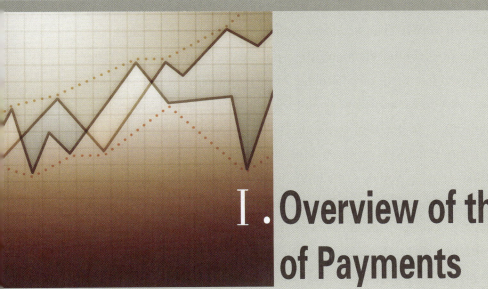

I. Overview of the Balance of Payments

(I) The Balance of Payments Environment

In 2016, China was facing a complex situation both domestically and externally. The global economy was recovering slowly, but there were more uncertainties in the global economic and political areas. The monetary policies of the various major advanced economies became further diversified. The Chinese domestic economy remained stable but structural contradictions continued to exist.

The global economy recovered slowly. The economic situation in the United States was relatively positive but after the presidential election future policies remained unclear. The situation in the Euro zone improved but it still faced problems due to the influx of refugees and banking-sector risks. The recovery in Japan was slow and there was less room to maneuver. The United Kingdom was stable after the Brexit referendum. However, the Brexit arrangements remained uncertain. The emerging markets grew steadily but still faced adjustment and transformation pressures(see Chart 1-1). According to the IMF's *World Economic Outlook,* released in January 2017, the advanced and emerging economies in 2016 were expected to grow by 1.6 percent and 4.1 percent, down 0.5 percentage point or even with the growth rate in 2015.

Global monetary policies further diversified. On December 14, 2016, the Fed announced an increase in the federal funds rate by 25 basis points, from 0.5 percent to 0.75 percent. The market expects that the Fed will gradually raise the rate due to the recovery of the macro economy. The ECB continued its QE policy on March 10, 2016 by cutting several rates and increasing asset purchasing in an expanding number of categories to stimulate economic growth and to improve inflation. Later, the ECB launched a package of monetary-easing measures. Unexpectedly, the Bank of Japan launched a negative rate policy on January 29, 2016 by adopting a three-tiered system, cutting the interest rate of the current accounts that financial institutions held at the BOJ from 0.1 percent to -0.1 percent. The Bank of England kept the benchmark rate and the scale of asset purchasing unchanged during the first half of 2016. After the Brexit referendum, the BOE implemented a package of stimulus measures, including cutting the benchmark rate and increasing asset purchasing. The emerging economies further diversified. The economies in Russia, India, Brazil, and Korea cut their benchmark rates to stimulate economic growth against external shocks. Other countries, such as South Africa, Colombia, Egypt, and Mexico, tightened their monetary policies against the rising inflationary pressures and the shock of the increase in the US rate.

Surging turbulence in international financial markets. In 2016, Black Swan events often occurred in the political, economic, and social arenas of international society. Populism, de-

Chart 1-1

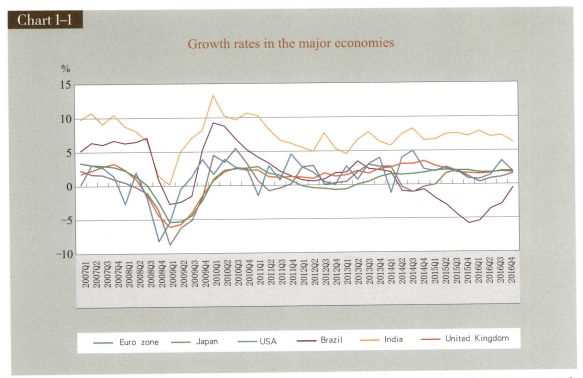

Growth rates in the major economies

Note: The US growth rate is the annualized quarterly growth rate; the growth rates of the other countries are the year-on-year quarterly growth rates.
Source: CEIC.

globalization, and trade investment protectionism caused a surge in geopolitical uncertainties and rising turbulence in the financial markets. In 2016, the USD index surged when the Euro, the British Pound, as well as the currencies in many emerging market depreciated against the USD, but the Japanese Yen appreciated against the USD. Treasury bond yields diversified in the major economies, and global stock markets as well as staple-goods markets experienced a popular rebound. The Dow Jones Industrial Average, the Euro Stoxx50, and the MSCI Emerging Markets Index increased by 13.4 percent, 0.7 percent, and 8.6 percent respectively, and the S&P GSCI increased by 27.8 percent (see Chart 1-2 and Chart 1-3).

The domestic economy operated smoothly. In 2016, the economy registered slower but stable performance, with a good momentum for growth. The structural reforms on the supply side made progress. GDP totaled USD 7.44 billion, representing growth of 6.7 percent year on year. The CPI grew by 2 percent (see Chart 1-4) and the employment rate remained stable. The quality of economic growth continued to improve, with the ratio of the service industry accounting for 52 percent of GDP and consumption contributing 62 percent of the total growth. Consumption in the emerging industries recorded rapid growth. In 2016, China continued

Chart 1–2

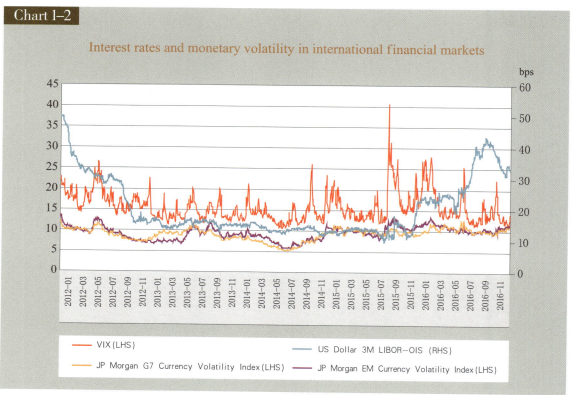

Interest rates and monetary volatility in international financial markets

Source: Bloomberg.

Chart 1–3

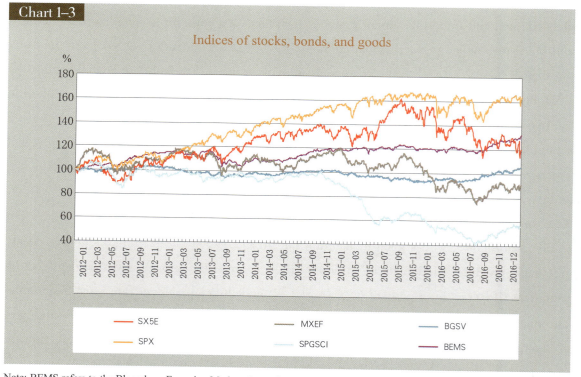

Indices of stocks, bonds, and goods

Note: BEMS refers to the Bloomberg Emerging Markets Sovereign Bond Index; BGSV refers to the Bloomberg Advanced Countries Sovereign Bond Index; MXEF refers to the MSCI Emerging Markets Index; SPX refers to Standard & Poor's 500 Index; SX5E refers to the Euro STOXX 50 Index; and SPGSCI refers to Standard & Poor's GSCI Index. 2012=100.
Source: Bloomberg.

Chart 1-4

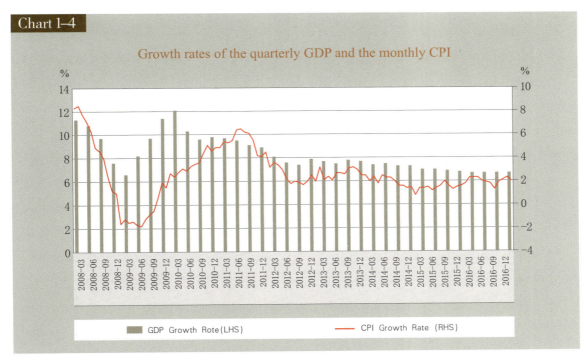

Growth rates of the quarterly GDP and the monthly CPI

Source: NBS.

its prudential monetary policy and also maintained sufficient flexibility to stabilize market expectations and to create proper monetary and financial environments for the structural reforms on the supply side. However, it should be noted that structural conflicts in the Chinese economy still remained problematic because investments by the private sector were insufficiently active and momentum for endogenous growth was weak. China was still facing challenges with respect to balancing among stable economic growth, asset bubble risks, and environmental protection.

Box 1

Positive Feedback from the Reform Policies to Realize Equilibrium

In the face of the complicated foreign-exchange market, the PBC and the SAFE realized that a favorable reform would focus on the reform of capital inflows, which would benefit the challenges from short-term risks of capital outflows and would help promote the long-term opening up of financial markets and the convertibility of the capital account. Such reforms would not only strongly promote the balance of payments situation and maintain a stable supply–demand relationship but would also further the opening up to serve the real economy.

The inter-bank bond market was opened to foreign investors, which indicated a new stage in capital account convertibility. In February 2016, the PBC released public notice No.3 of 2016, announcing an expansion of the list of foreign institutional investors to allow more categories of foreign investors to legally invest in the inter–bank bond market. In May 2016, it was announced that foreign investors in the inter–bank bond market should register with the SAFE. There is no upper limit for such investments. Foreign investors should maintain a balance between their currency inflows and currency outflows to avoid a BOP shock due to either massive capital inflows or massive capital outflows. By the end of December 2016, over 180 foreign institutions or their products had filed with the Shanghai headquarters of the PBC, thus improving the opening up of the inter–bank market. Since March 2016, outstanding domestic bond assets held by nonresidents have surged, amounting to CNY 870 billion by the end of 2016 (see Chart C1–1). The needs of market participants to take full advantage of both the domestic and the international markets and of resources both at home and overseas were better served.

Comprehensive macro prudential regulation of cross-border financing was carried out in the entire country to facilitate cross-border financing by market participants. To establish a comprehensive macro prudential regulatory framework for external debts and capital flows is an important strategy in the Thirteenth Five–Year Plan and a crucial measure to deepen the reform of foreign administration and to promote facilitation of trade and investment. In January 2016, as a pilot program, twenty–seven financial institutions and enterprises in the four free–trade zones were authorized to finance from abroad, with an upper limit under a certain ratio of their capital or net assets. In May 2016, the policy was further carried out in the entire country after making adjustments according to the experience of the pilot program to alleviate the problem of difficult and expansive financing. Beginning in the second quarter of 2016, China's outstanding external debt rebounded (see Chart C1–2).

QFII and RQFII regulations were reformed to create a favorable investment environment for foreign investors. In February and August of 2016, QFII and RQFII foreign–exchange regulations were reformed respectively by increasing the upper limit of the QFII/RQFII quota, simplifying the administrative process, facilitating capital inflows and outflows, and shortening the lock–up period. The reforms helped to enhance the

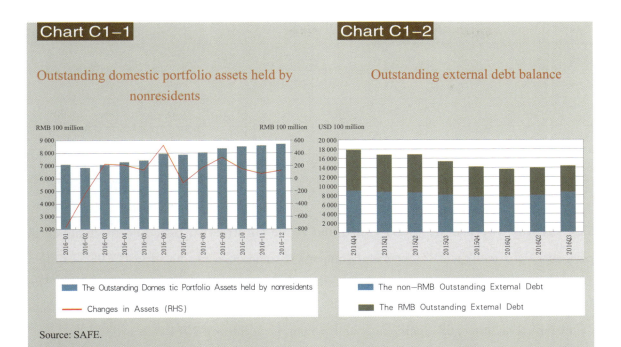

Chart C1-1

Outstanding domestic portfolio assets held by nonresidents

Chart C1-2

Outstanding external debt balance

Source: SAFE.

consistency of foreign–exchange regulation of QFIIs and RQFIIs as well as to promote the opening up of the domestic capital market. Moreover, the reforms facilitated cross–border portfolio investments as well as cross–border financing and investments. By the end of 2016, 278 QFII institutions had been approved, with a QFII quota of USD 87.3 billion, and 177 RQFII institutions had been approved, with a QFII quota of CNY 528.5 billion.

Regulations regarding the sale of foreign exchange under the capital account were reformed to better balance between supply and demand in the foreign-exchange market. In June 2016, the reform of voluntary foreign–exchange external–debt settlements external were carried out throughout the country and the voluntary foreign–exchange settlement policy was unified under the capital account. In addition, the negative list of capital account receipts and settlement purposes was cut. The reform further satisfied and facilitated business and capital operations of domestic enterprises as well as their cross–border investments and financing.

(II) The Main Characteristics of the Balance of Payments

During 2016, the current account surplus totaled USD 196.4 billion, down by 35 percent year on year. The non–reserve financial account deficit totaled USD 417 billion, down by 4 percent year on year (see Table 1–1).

Table 1-1 Structure of the BOP surplus

Unit: USD 100 million

Items	2010	2011	2012	2013	2014	2015	2016
Current account balance	2 378	1 361	2 154	1 482	2 360	3 042	1 964
As a % of the GDP	3.9%	1.8%	2.5%	1.5%	2.3%	2.7%	1.8%
Capital and financial account balance	2 822	2 600	-360	3 430	-514	-4 345	-4 170
As a % of the GDP	4.6%	3.4%	-0.4%	3.6%	-0.5%	-3.9%	-3.7%

Sources: SAFE, NBS.

The surplus of trade in goods continued to be significant. Based on the balance of payments statistics,[①] in 2016 exports and imports of trade in goods totaled USD 1 989.5 billion and USD 1 495.4 billion, down by 7 percent and 5 percent respectively year on year. The surplus of trade in goods amounted to USD 494.1 billion, down by 14 percent year on year from the historical high but still significantly higher than the surplus in 2014 and earlier.

Growth of the deficit in trade in services slowed down. In 2016, trade in services revenue totaled USD 208.4 billion, down by 4 percent year on year. Trade in services expenditures amounted to USD 452.6 billion, up by 4 percent. Trade in services recorded a deficit of USD 244.2 billion, up by 12 percent yearonyear. In particular, the travel deficit totaled USD 216.7 billion, a growth rate of 6 percent, 6 percentage points lower than the growth rate in 2015 (see Chart 1–5).

The deficit in primary income[②] was sustained. In 2016, revenue and expenditures of primary income amounted to USD 225.8 billion and USD 269.8 billion respectively, up by 1 percent and 2 percent. Primary income posted a deficit of USD 44 billion, up by 7 percent. In particular, employee compensation recorded a surplus of USD 20.7 billion, down by 25 percent year on year. Investment income posted a deficit of USD 65 billion, down by 6 percent (see Chart 1–5). In terms of investment income, outward investment income totaled USD 198.4 billion, up by 5 percent, and profits and dividends of inward investments totaled USD 263.4

---

① The BOP statistics and the statistics of the General Administration of Customs with respect to trade in goods can be reconciled by the following: First, trade in goods in the BOP records transactions when the transfer of the ownership of goods (such as ordinary trade and processing trade goods with imported materials) and transactions without ownership transfers (such as processing trade with customer materials and outward processing) are regarded as trade in services instead of trade in goods. Second, the BOP records imports and exports based on FOB, whereas the General Administration of Customs records exports based on FOB but it records imports based on CIF. Thus, the BOP statistics deduct insurance and freight from the value of imports and add them to the trade in services. Third, information on repatriations is included. Fourth, net exports of goods under the turnover of goods, which are collected by the General Administration of Customs, are included.

② The IMF's *Balance of Payments and International Investment Manual* (Sixth Edition) renamed the income item under the current account as primary income and renamed current transfers as secondary income.

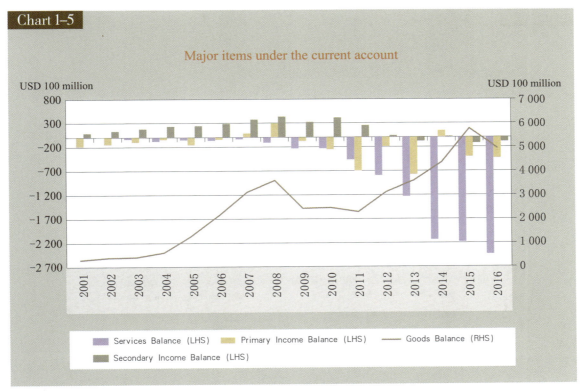

Chart 1-5

Major items under the current account

USD 100 million

USD 100 million

Services Balance (LHS)   Primary Income Balance (LHS)   ——— Goods Balance (RHS)
Secondary Income Balance (LHS)

Source: SAFE.

billion, up by 2 percent.

The deficit in secondary income decreased. In 2016, revenue and expenditures of secondary income amounted to USD 30.9 billion and USD 40.4 billion respectively, down by 14 percent and 17 percent. The deficit in secondary income amounted to USD 9.5 billion, a decrease of 25 percent (see Chart 1–5).

Direct investments recorded a deficit. Based on the BOP statistics, in 2016 direct investments[①] recorded a deficit of USD 46.6 billion, whereas in 2015 they recorded a surplus of USD 68.1 billion (see Chart 1–6). In particular, direct investment assets recorded a net increase of USD 217.2 billion, up by 25 percent year on year, and direct investment liabilities recorded a net increase of USD 170.6 billion, down by 30 percent.

The deficit in portfolio investments decreased. In 2016, the deficit in portfolio investments amounted to USD 62.2 billion, down by 6 percent year on year (see Chart 1–6). In particular, outward portfolio investments recorded a net outflow of USD 103.4 billion, up by 41 percent,

---

① Unlike the data released by the Ministry of Commerce, direct investments based on the BOP statistics also include unpaid and unremitted profits, retained earnings, shareholder loans, foreign capital utilized by financial institutions, and real estate purchases by nonresidents.

Chart 1–6

Major items under the capital and financial account

Sources: SAFE.

Chart 1–7

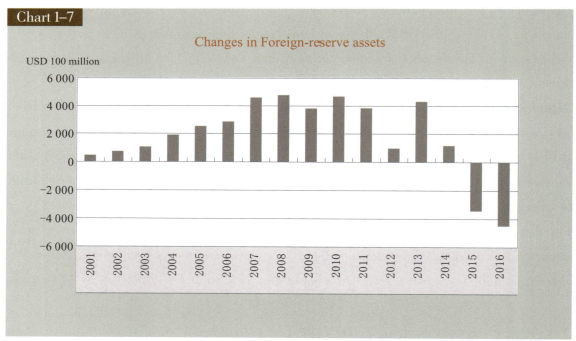

Changes in Foreign-reserve assets

Sources: SAFE.

and inward portfolio investments recorded a net inflow of USD 41.2 billion, up by 512 percent.

The deficit in other investments deceased notably. In 2016, other investments, such as loans, trade in credits, and deposits, posted a deficit of USD 303.5 billion, down by 30 percent year on year (see Chart 1–6). In particular, China's outward other investments recorded a net increase of USD 333.6 billion, up by 305 percent, and inward other investments recorded a net increase of USD 30.1 billion, whereas in 2015 they recorded a net decrease of USD 351.5 billion.

Reserve assets continued to drop. In 2016, reserve assets involving transactions (excluding the effects of non–transactional values, such as the exchange rate and prices) decreased by USD 443.7 billion. In particular, foreign–reserve assets involving transactions decreased by USD 448.7 billion (see Chart 1–7). By the end of 2016, China's foreign–reserveassets totaled USD 3010.5 billion.

Table 1-2 Balance of payments in 2016
Unit：USD 100 million

Item	Line No.	2016
1. Current account	1	1 964
Credit	2	24 546
Debit	3	-22 583
1.A Goods and services	4	2 499
Credit	5	21 979
Debit	6	-19 480
1.A.a Goods	7	4 941
Credit	8	19 895
Debit	9	-14 954
1.A.b Services	10	-2 442
Credit	11	2 084
Debit	12	-4 526
1.A.b.1 Manufacturing services on physical inputs owned by others	13	184
Credit	14	185
Debit	15	-2
1.A.b.2 Maintenance and repair services n.i.e	16	32
Credit	17	52
Debit	18	-20
1.A.b.3 Transport	19	-468
Credit	20	338
Debit	21	-806
1.A.b.4 Travel	22	-2 167
Credit	23	444
Debit	24	-2 611
1.A.b.5 Construction	25	42
Credit	26	127
Debit	27	-85
1.A.b.6 Insurance and pension services	28	-88
Credit	29	41
Debit	30	-129
1.A.b.7 Financial services	31	11
Credit	32	32

(continued)

Item	Line No.	2016
Debit	33	-20
1.A.b.8 Charges for the use of intellectual property	34	-228
Credit	35	12
Debit	36	-240
1.A.b.9 Telecommunications, computer, and information services	37	127
Credit	38	254
Debit	39	-127
1.A.b.10 Other business services	40	147
Credit	41	580
Debit	42	-432
1.A.b.11 Personal, cultural, and recreational services	43	-14
Credit	44	7
Debit	45	-21
1.A.b.12 Government goods and services n.i.e	46	-20
Credit	47	12
Debit	48	-32
1.B Primary income	49	-440
Credit	50	2 258
Debit	51	-2 698
1.B.1 Compensation of employees	52	207
Credit	53	269
Debit	54	-62
1.B.2 Investment income	55	-650
Credit	56	1 984
Debit	57	-2 634
1.B.3 Other primary income	58	3
Credit	59	6
Debit	60	-2
1.C Secondary income	61	-95
Credit	62	309
Debit	63	-404
2. Capital and financial account	64	263
2.1 Capital account	65	-3
Credit	66	3
Debit	67	-7
2.2 Financial account	68	267
Assets	69	-2 174
Liabilities	70	2 441
2.2.1 Financial account excluding reserve assets	71	-4 170
Financial assets excluding reserve assets	72	-6 611
Liabilities	73	2 441
2.2.1.1 Direct investment	74	-466
2.2.1.1.1 Assets	75	-2 172
2.2.1.1.1.1 Equity and investment fund shares	76	-1 484
2.2.1.1.1.2 Debt instruments	77	-688
2.2.1.1.2 Liabilities	78	1 706
2.2.1.1.2.1 Equity and investment fund shares	79	1 642
2.2.1.1.2.2 Debt instruments	80	64
2.2.1.2 Portfolio investment	81	-622
2.2.1.2.1 Assets	82	-1 034
2.2.1.2.1.1 Equity and investment fund shares	83	-385
2.2.1.2.1.2 Debt securities	84	-649
2.2.1.2.2 Liabilities	85	412
2.2.1.2.2.1 Equity and investment fund shares	86	189
2.2.1.2.2.2 Debt securities	87	223

(continued)

Item	Line No.	2016
2.2.1.3 Financial derivatives (other than reserves) and employee stock options	88	-47
2.2.1.3.1 Assets	89	-69
2.2.1.3.2 Liabilities	90	22
2.2.1.4 Other investment	91	-3 035
2.2.1.4.1 Assets	92	-3 336
2.2.1.4.1.1 Other equity	93	0
2.2.1.4.1.2 Currency and deposits	94	-435
2.2.1.4.1.3 Loans	95	-1 147
2.2.1.4.1.4 Insurance, pension, and standardized guarantee schemes	96	-3
2.2.1.4.1.5 Trade credit and advances	97	-1 008
2.2.1.4.1.6 Other accounts receivable	98	-743
2.2.1.4.2 Liabilities	99	301
2.2.1.4.2.1 Other equity	100	0
2.2.1.4.2.2 Currency and deposits	101	102
2.2.1.4.2.3 Loans	102	-196
2.2.1.4.2.4 Insurance, pension, and standardized guarantee schemes	103	-6
2.2.1.4.2.5 Trade credit and advances	104	162
2.2.1.4.2.6 Other accounts payable	105	239
2.2.1.4.2.7 Special drawing rights	106	0
2.2.2 Reserve assets	107	4 437
2.2.2.1 Monetary gold	108	0
2.2.2.2 Special drawing rights	109	3
2.2.2.3 Reserve position in the IMF	110	-53
2.2.2.4 Foreign exchange reserves	111	4 487
2.2.2.5 Other reserve assets	112	0
3.Net errors and omissions	113	-2 227

Notes: 1. This chart was compiled according to Balance of Payments and International Investment Position Manual Six Edition.
2. In the financial account, a positive value for assets indicates a net decrease, whereas a negative value indicates a net increase. A positive value for liabilities indicates a net increase, whereas a negative value indicates a net decrease.
3.The chart is based on a rounding principle.
Source: SAFE.

(III) Evaluation of the Balance of Payments

The surplus in the current account was at a reasonable level. In 2016, the ratio of China's current account surplus to GDP was 1.8 percent, down by 0.9 percentage point year on year and it remained at a reasonable level. In particular, the ratio of the surplus of trade in goods to GDP was 4.4 percent, down by 0.8 percentage point, and the ratio of the deficit in trade in services to GDP was 2.2 percent, up by 0.2 percentage point. The ratio of the total deficit of primary and secondary income to GDP was 0.5 percent (see Chart 1-8).

Pressures on capital outflows were alleviated. In 2016, the deficit in the non-reserve financial account totaled USD 417 billion, down by 4 percent. In particular, the deficit was

Chart 1–8

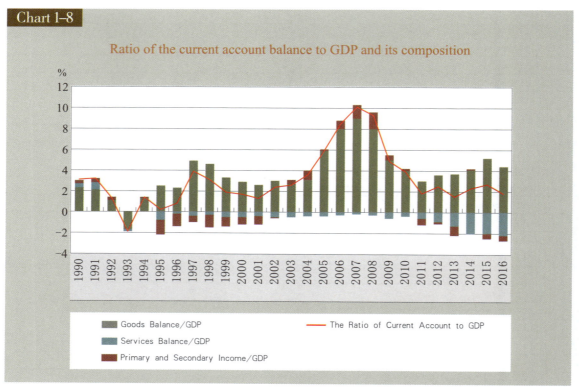

Sources: SAFE, NBS.

Chart 1–9

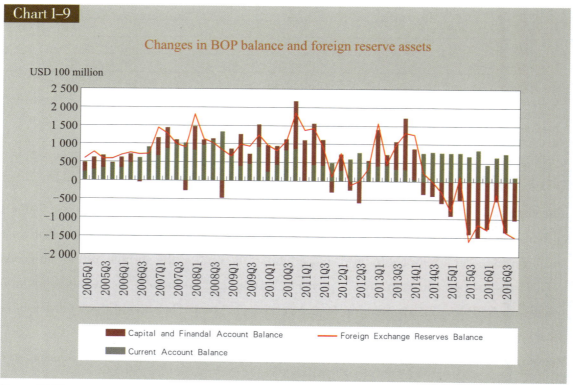

Sources: SAFE.

USD 126.3 billion in the first quarter, far less than the deficit in the fourth quarter of 2015 (USD 150.4 billion). In the second quarter, the deficit decreased notably to USD 52.4 billion. But in the third quarter, the deficit rebounded to USD 135.1 billion, the highest quarterly deficit in 2016. In the fourth quarter, the deficit decreased to USD 103.1, down by 31 percent(see Chart1−9).

Domestic entities continued to increase their external assets. In 2016, domestic entities became more diversified in terms of overseas investments, and outward direct investments, portfolio investments, and other investments all showed an upward momentum. China's external assets recorded a net increase of USD 661.1 billion, up by 98 percent year on year. In particular, the net increase in outward direct investments totaled USD 217.2 billion, up by 25 percent and accounting for 33 percent of the total net increase in outward investments, down by 19 percentage points year on year. Outward portfolio investments recorded a net outflow of USD 103.4 billion, up by 41 percent and accounting for 16 percent of the total, down by 6 percentage points. Other investment assets, including loans and deposits, recorded a net increase of USD 333.6 billion, up by 305 percent and accounting for 50 percent of the total, up by 25 percentage points(see Chart 1−10).

External liabilities changed from a net outflow to a net inflow. In 2016, the net inflow of inward investments (the increase in external liabilities), including inward direct investments, portfolio investments, and other investments, totaled USD 244.1 billion, whereas in 2015

Chart 1–10

The structure of cross-border capital flows in 2016

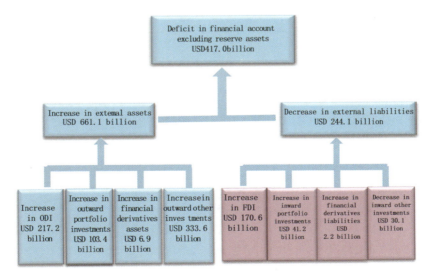

Source: SAFE.

inward investments posted a net outflow of USD 101 billion. In particular, the first quarter recorded a net outflow of USD 13.5 billion. Beginning in the second quarter, it changed to a net inflow with an upward momentum, and the net quarterly inflow totaled USD 77.1 billion, USD 84.2 billion, and USD 96.3 billion respectively(see Chart 1–11). Inward direct investments maintained a net inflow of USD 170.6 billion, among which the second half of the year recorded a net inflow of USD 95.8 billion, up by 28 percent from the net inflow during the first half of the year. Inward portfolio investments recorded a net inflow of USD 41.2 billion, up by 512 percent year on year, indicating a more attractive and deeper domestic securities market. Moreover, other investments posted a net inflow of USD 30.1 billion, whereas in 2015 they recorded a net outflow of USD 351.5 billion, indicating that the repayment of external liabilities by domestic entities had ended and the need of domestic entities for external financing had rebounded.

Pressures on capital outflows came from domestic entities but overall risks remained controllable. In 2016, China's external debt resumed its increasing trend, and the main source of capital outflows came from domestic entities increasing their external assets in terms of direct investments, portfolio investments, and loans. From 2014 to 2016, the increase in outward investments totaled nearly USD 1.5 trillion, which equaled the eight-year accumulation prior to 2013. In 2016, the increase totaled USD 661.1 billion. This indicated a strengthening of comprehensive national power, an enhancement of enterprise competitiveness,

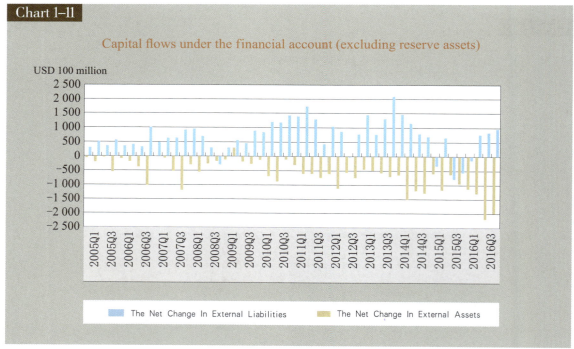

Chart 1–11

Sources: SAFE.

and an increasing demand for asset diversification. The rapid growth of the external assets of domestic entities had a short-term impact on China's BOP equilibrium, causing some irrational or abnormal activities. In general, China's BOP risks were well under control and were able to guard against and adapt to the adjustments due to the relatively high economic growth rate, the sound fiscal situation, the prudent financial system, the sustained current account surplus, and the sufficient foreign reserves. However, attention should still be paid to the related risks.

Box 2

An Objective Perspective on China's Foreign-Exchange Reserves and Their Fluctuations

By the end of 2016, China's outstanding foreign-exchange reserves totaled USD 3010.5 billion, which was still high even though it had declined from its historical high. The fluctuations still need to be evaluated from an objective perspective.

China's foreign-exchange reserves remained the highest in the world. China ranks as number 1 in terms of foreign reserves, followed by Japan (USD 1.16 trillion) and Switzerland (USD 634.9 billion). The outstanding foreign-exchange reserves of Brazil, India, and Russia were about USD 300 billion (see Chart C2-1). China accounted for 28 percent of the global foreign-exchange reserves (USD 10.7 trillion), and Japan and Switzerland accounted for 11 percent and 6 percent respectively.

In terms of external payments and liability reimbursements, China's foreign-exchange reserves were sufficient. There is no unified standard for foreign-exchange reserve adequacy. According to traditional standards, a country's foreign-exchange reserves should be sufficient for at least three months of imports. Supposing there are no RMB payments, they should amount to at least USD 400 billion in China. In terms of external debt reimbursements, a country's foreign-exchange reserves should cover 100 percent of its short-term external debt. China's outstanding short-term external debt (including both its foreign-exchange debt and its RMB debt) totaled USD 800-900 billion, down from that which was outstanding at the end of 2014 (USD 1.3 trillion), which indicated that the pressures for external debt reimbursements had been notably alleviated. In general, China's foreign-exchange reserve position was adequate in terms of

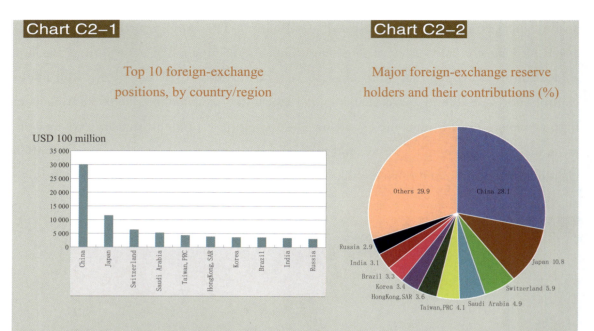

Chart C2–1

Top 10 foreign-exchange positions, by country/region

USD 100 million

Chart C2–2

Major foreign-exchange reserve holders and their contributions (%)

China 28.1
Others 29.9
Russia 2.9
India 3.1
Brazil 3.3
Korea 3.4
HongKong,SAR 3.6
Taiwan,PRC 4.1
Saudi Arabia 4.9
Switzerland 5.9
Japan 10.8

international payments and debt reimbursements as well as in terms of ensuring economic and financial security.

In terms of meeting the needs of domestic entities for external assets, the adjustment in the foreign-exchange reserve position reflected the gradual and positive structural adjustments for the holders of external assets. In recent years, the demand for asset diversification from the private sector has been growing due to the increasing income of domestic enterprises and individuals. According to China's IIP statistics, by the end of 2016 the external asset position of the private sector accounted for 52 percent of the total, which, for the first time, accounted for over one–half of the external asset position. At the end of 2016, China's private sector had a net foreign debt of 1 300 billion dollars, which was significantly lower than the highest of 2 300 billion dollars at the end of 2014. The external assets of the private sector were better matched with their liabilities. In addition, foreign–exchange reserves are not the only source to satisfy the needs of the private sector for external assets. The sustained current account surplus and the policies to facilitate capital inflows, including cross–border financing and the opening up of the market, also became sources of the increase in external assets. However, the adjustment in the external assets between the official side and the private side should be reasonable and consistent with the economic development and opening up. China will increase RMB exchange–rate flexibility and keep the exchange rate stable at a reasonable and equilibrium level and it will further improve the administration of cross–border capital flows under a macro prudential framework, which will smooth the adjustments.

The recent adjustment of foreign-exchange reserves was driven by factors such as market operations, price adjustments, and the diversification of foreign-reserve investments. First, the central bank intervened in the foreign–exchange market to satisfy the need of domestic entities for outward investments, such as direct investments, portfolio investments, and loans. Since the second half of 2014, the above investments increased by over USD 1.2 trillion. In addition, the intervention also met the need for the outflow of other investments, including portfolio investments and external debt, which totaled USD 270 billion in terms of net outflows. In particular, from the second half of 2014 to the first quarter year of 2016, cumulative net outflows totaled USD 400 billion, whereas in the flowing three quarters of 2016 cumulative net inflows totaled USD 130 billion. Second, the reevaluation of asset priceswas another factor driving the fluctuations in the foreign–exchange reserve asset position. Third, the exchange rate of other currencies against the USD may cause fluctuations in the foreign–exchange reserve position since the USD is the currency denomination. Fourth, according to the IMF's definition of foreign–exchange reserves, foreign–exchange reserves that used to support going–out investments will be moved out of the total reserve position, and vice versa.

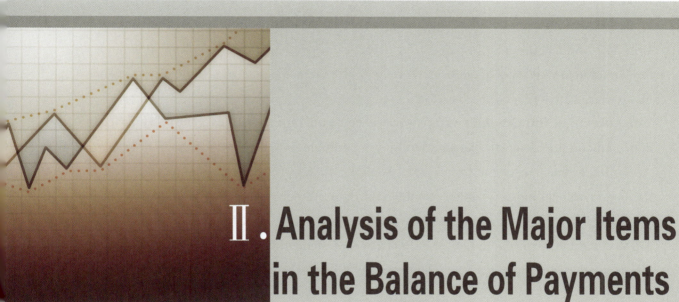

II. Analysis of the Major Items in the Balance of Payments

(I) Trade in Goods

The decrease in exports and imports of trade in goods slowed down, and the dependence on foreign trade continued to decline. According to the statistics of the General Administration of Customs, in 2016 China's exports declined by 8 percent and its imports declined by 5 percent. Export and imports totaled USD 3.7 trillion, down by 7 percent, a year–on–year decline of 1.3 percentage points. The surplus of trade in goods amounted to USD 510.7 billion, down by 14 percent. In 2016, China's foreign trade dependence (the ratio of foreign trade to GDP) was 33 percent, down by 3 percentage points and representing a decline for six consecutive years (see Chart 2–1).

The volume of imports and exports increased and import prices gradually rose. In 2016, rebounding domestic demand led to a remarkable increase in the volume of imports. According to the statistics of the General Administration of Customs (denominated in RMB), the import volume index recorded monthly growth of 3.7 percent in 2016 and 4.4 percent in Q4, reflecting that the domestic economy had gradually stabilized. In addition, from August to December of 2016, the import price index recorded monthly growth of 2.7 percent due to the fluctuations in staple goods, including energy prices, whereas it had recorded a 7 percent

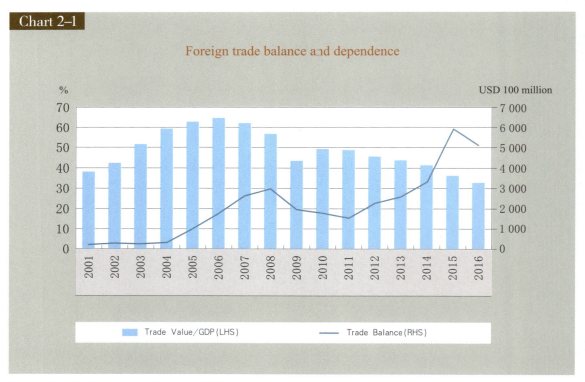

Chart 2–1

Foreign trade balance and dependence

Sources: General Administration of Customs, NBS.

monthly decrease prior to August. Moreover, the volume of exports increased by 2.7 percent monthly and export prices decreased by 2.2 percent monthly.

The surplus of trade in goods grew, with a significant increase in foreign exchange net inflows. In 2016, China's trade in goods revenue and payments decreased by 9 percent and 13 percent respectively, causing a surplus of USD 263.6 billion, up by 25 percent. In particular, the trade in goods surplus settled with foreign exchange totaled USD 257.9 billion, accounting for 98 percent of the total surplus of trade in goods, whereas in 2015 the foreign exchange surplus of trade in goods was USD 36.4 billion. The surplus of trade in goods settled with RMB totaled USD 5.7 billion, accounting for 2 percent of the total surplus of trade in goods. In 2015, it totaled USD 175.3 billion.

Privately-owned enterprises contributed more to the surplus than they had in the past, and contributions by foreign-funded enterprises declined slightly. In 2016, privately-owned enterprises recorded a surplus of trade in goods of USD 496.8 billion, down by 12 percent year on year and accounting for 97 percent of the total surplus, a decrease of 3 percentage points. Foreign-funded enterprises recorded a surplus of USD 146.5 billion, down by 16 percent and accounting for 29 percent of the total, a slight decrease of 1 percentage

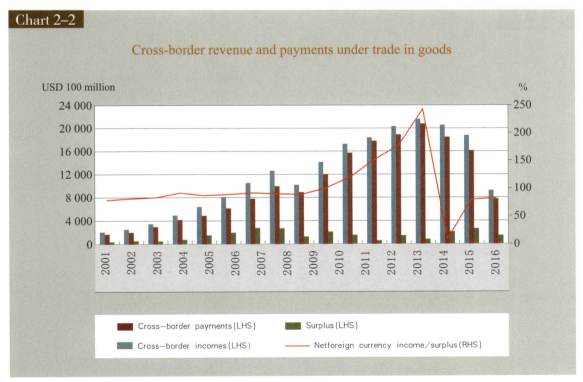

Chart 2–2

Cross-border revenue and payments under trade in goods

Source: SAFE.

Chart 2–3

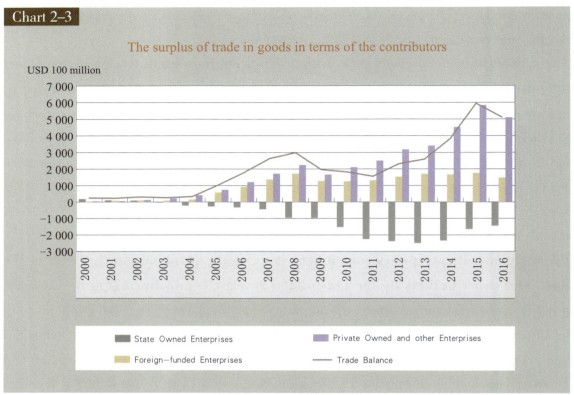

The surplus of trade in goods in terms of the contributors

Source: General Administration of Customs.

Chart 2–4

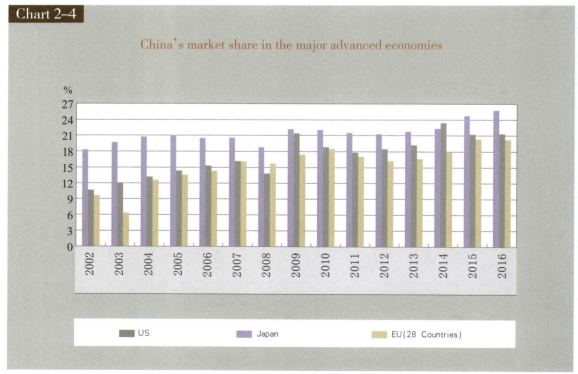

China's market share in the major advanced economies

Source: CEIC.

point year on year. State-owned enterprises posted a deficit of USD 145.2 billion, down by 12 percent year on year (see Chart 2–3).

China's exports to the major advanced economies remained stable. In 2016, US imports from China accounted for 21 percent of its total imports, down by 0.4 percentage point. EU imports from China accounted for 20 percent of its total imports, which remained constant with that in 2015. Japan's imports from China accounted for 26 percent of its total, up by 1 percentage point year on year.

(II) Trade in Services

Trade in services maintained rapid growth, especially that of high value-added trade in services. In 2016, China's trade in services totaled USD 661 billion, up by 1 percent, whereas trade in goods totaled USD 3485 billion, which represented a year–on–year decrease of 6 percent. The ratio of trade in services to trade in goods was 19 percent, up by 1 percentage point year on year (see Chart 2–5). High value–added trade in services outperformed traditional trade in services. In 2016, processing manufacturing services and transportation, which are both traditional trade in services, declined by 9 percent and 8 percent respectively.

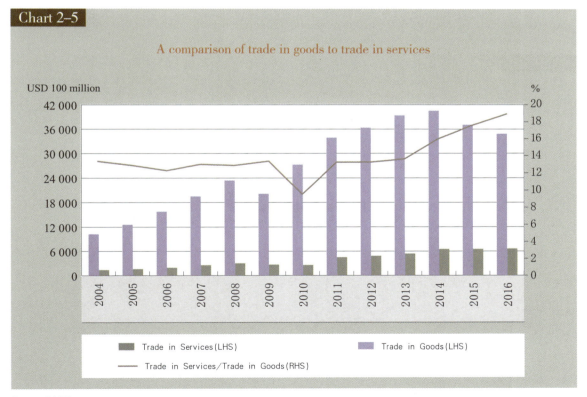

Chart 2–5

A comparison of trade in goods to trade in services

Source: SAFE.

High value–added trade in services, such as telecommunications, computer and information services, entertainment, and charges for the use of intellectual property all increased by over 6 percent year on year. China's trade in services continued to be upgraded due to the related policy support.

Trade in services revenue declined. In 2016, trade in services revenue totaled USD 208.4 billion, down by 4 percent year on year (see Chart 2–6). Among the major items, travel revenue dropped slightly by 1 percent. Transportation, manufacturing services, and other business services (including R&D transfers, commissioned R&D, and professional and consultancy services such as legal services, accounting, and advertisements) declined by 12 percent, 9 percent, and 1 percent respectively.

Trade in services expenditures grew slightly. In 2016, trade in services expenditures totaled USD 452.6 billion, up by 4 percent year on year. Among the major items, travel accounted for 58 percent of total expenditures, 1 percentage point higher than the ratio in 2015. Travel expenditures grew by 5 percent year on year, but the growth rate decreased by 5 percentage points. Transport accounted for 18 percent of the total, 2 percentage points lower than the ratio in 2015. Transportation spending declined by 6 percent year on year, 5 percentage points less than the decline in 2015. Other business services and charges for the use of intellectual property grew significantly by 9 percent year on year, whereas in 2015 they recorded a decline

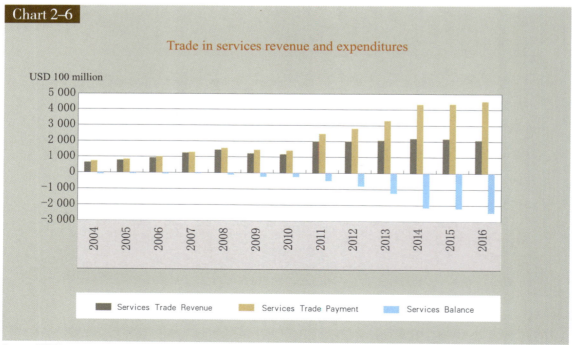

Chart 2–6

Trade in services revenue and expenditures

USD 100 million

Services Trade Revenue   Services Trade Payment   Services Balance

Source: SAFE.

of 3 percent.

The deficit in trade in services increased. In 2016, the trade in services deficit totaled USD 244.2 billion, up by 12 percent year on year, 10 percentage points higher than the growth rate in 2015 (see Chart2–7). The travel deficit totaled USD 216.7 billion, up by 6 percent year on year, 6 percentage points lower than the growth rate in 2015. With improved economic development and national income, more Chinese go abroad to travel and study, facilitated by globalization and related policies. After a period of high–speed growth in overseas travel and study from 2009 to 2013, the growth rate of the travel deficit decelerated with the released demand.

Deficit counterparties were highly concentrated. In 2016, China's top ten partners in terms of trade in services were Hong Kong SAR, the United States, Japan, Korea, the United Kingdom, Germany, Canada, Australia, Singapore, and Taiwan PRC. Trade in services with these countries amounted to USD 449.8 billion, accounting for 68 percent of the total. In particular, with the exception of Singapore, China posted deficits with nine of them. China's deficit with six partners totaled over USD 10 billion (see Chart 2–8). In particular, the United States ranked as the number one top deficit partner, followed by Hong Kong SAR, Canada, Australia, Japan, and the United Kingdom. Compared with 2015, China's deficit with the Hong Kong SAR, the United States, Japan, Korea, the United Kingdom, Canada, Australia,

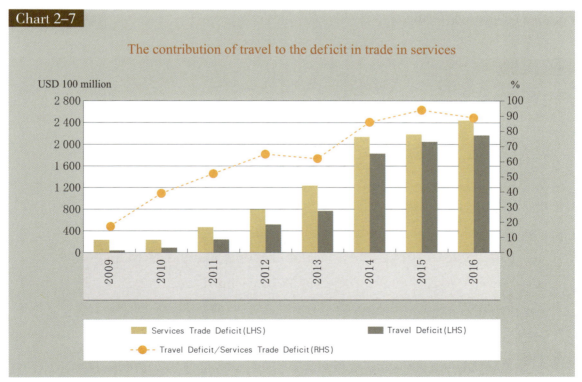

Chart 2–7

The contribution of travel to the deficit in trade in services

Services Trade Deficit (LHS)　　Travel Deficit (LHS)
- - Travel Deficit/Services Trade Deficit (RHS)

Source: SAFE.

Chart 2–8

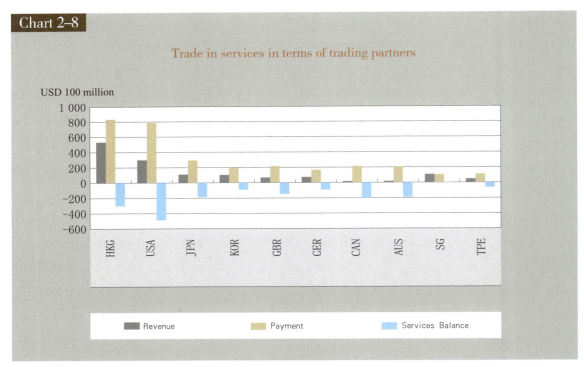

Trade in services in terms of trading partners

Source: SAFE.

and Germany increased, whereas the deficit with Taiwan PRC decreased and the surplus with Singapore increased slightly.

Box 3

Comprehensive Use of Payment Channel Data to Improve International Travel Statistics

Among the twelve types of trade in services, travel plays an important role in China's balance-of-payments statistics. Progressively improving the data sources, the SAFE thoroughly used the instruments to pay for both travel credits and debits in the balance of payments in 2016. It also revised the historical data for 2014 and 2015. As a result, China's travel credits and debits in 2016 declined from preliminary USD 118.2 billion and USD 341.2 billion respectively to USD 44.4 billion and USD 261.1 billion respectively, and accordingly the deficit declined slightly from USD 223.1 billion to USD 216.7 billion.

I. The coverage of travel

According to the IMF's *Balance of Payments and International Investment Position Manual, Sixth Edition (BPM6)*, travel covers goods and services acquired for one's own use or to be given away from an economy by nonresidents during their visits to that economy. Two points should be highlighted. First, nonresident travelers include both individuals who travel abroad for business or for personal purposes for a duration of less than one year, and individuals who study or undertake medical care abroad regardless of the duration of their visits. Nonresident travelers also include cross-border, seasonal, and other short-term workers whose expenses in an economy, other than their own, should be included under travel services. Second, although listed as a type of service, travel covers both goods and services acquired by nonresident travelers. Unlike other types of services, travel possesses a special feature in that it aims to collect traveler-related transactions, which cover broad types of goods and services such as transport and insurance acquired by travelers. Basically, all expenses for food and beverages, accommodations, and transport, entertainment, and consumption, living costs, and tuition fees should be covered by travel.

Table C3-1   The components of travel

1.A.b.4 Travel
1.A.b.4.1Business travel
1.A.b.4.1.1 Goods and services acquired by cross-border, seasonal, and other short-term workers
1.A.b.4.1.2 Other
1.A.b.4.2 Personal travel
1.A.b.4.2.1 Health-related travel
1.A.b.4.2.2 Education-related travel
1.A.b.4.2.3 Other

Source: *Balance of Payments and International Investment Position Manual (Sixth Edition)*.

II. Approaches to measure travel

Due to the broad coverage of travel in terms of the involved travelers, the types of transactions, and the variety of goods and services acquired, it is a challenge to fully cover travel by statistical means. Internationally, four approaches can be used to measure travel expenses. The first approach is based on the instruments used to pay for travel, and the most common instruments are credit and debit cards. The second approach uses surveys on business travel and individual travelers as well as the cross–border flows of travelers. The third approach uses data from partner economies. The fourth approach uses a data model. The four approaches can be used either individually or together.

III. Statistical methodology for travel in China

Historically, China used different approaches to compile travel statistics, including surveys on enterprises and individual travelers, data from partner economies, instruments to pay for travel, and a data model. As the SAFE established cross–border bank card statistics in 2014 and began to survey the ratio of cash expenses to total expenses in international travel in 2016, it was able to measure travel based on the payment instruments. As a result, the SAFE used this approach to compile travel in the balance of payments for 2016. The instruments cover credit and debit cards, international remittances, and cash. Among the instruments, payments by cards and by international remittances are fully covered by the SAFE. Based on an annual survey of the ratio of cash expenses to total expenses by individual travelers, the SAFE estimates the cash expenses for travel. Moreover, for transactions reported as travel but indeed are investments, such as property investments and financial types of insurance, the SAFE managed to restore the transactions to the appropriate accounts based on the available information. After adopting the new approach, China can compile travel credits and debitsin a more compatible way. The improvements help enhance the coverage, expand the statistical dimensions, and make it possible to compile travel data by country/area.

(III) Direct Investments

Direct investments changed from net inflows to net outflows. [1] Based on the BOP statistics, in 2016 China's direct investments recorded a net outflow of USD 46.6 billion (see Chart 2–9), whereas in 2015 they recorded a net inflow of USD 68.1 billion. There were two reasons behind this change in the direct investment balance from continued inflows to net outflows. On the one hand, more Chinese enterprises were going out for the purpose of allocating global

---

[1] The net flow of direct investments refers to the gap between the net increase in direct investment assets and the net increase in direct investment liabilities. When the net increase in direct investment assets is more than the net increase in direct investment liabilities, a net outflow is recorded, and vice versa.

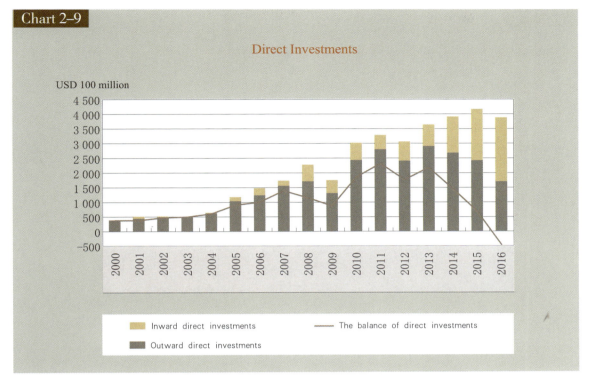

| Chart 2–9 |

Direct Investments

USD 100 million

Legend:
- Inward direct investments
- Outward direct investments
- The balance of direct investments

Source: SAFE.

resources. On the other hand, net inflows of inward direct investments decreased significantly. However, China's direct investments in Q4 changed to net inflows, with more rational outward investments and more inward direct investment inflows.

Direct investment assets[①] increased. In 2016, China's direct investment assets (mainly China's outward direct investments) recorded a net increase of USD 217.2 billion, up by 25 percent year on year (see Chart 2–10). After the net increase in direct investment assets exceeded USD 100 billion for the first time in 2014, it took only two years for China to record a net increase in direct investment assets of USD 200 billion. China's direct investment assets grew rapidly due to economic development. First, the growing comprehensive national power led to the rapid growth of outward investments. China has changed from a capital inflow stage to a capital outflow stage and from goods exports to both goods exports and capital exports together. Second, the demand for the allocation of global resources was also surging. Chinese enterprises were more willing to enter international markets. The Belt and Road initiative and

---

① A major component of direct investment assets is outward direct investments. In addition, reverse investments by domestic foreign-funded enterprises to their parent companies are also included.

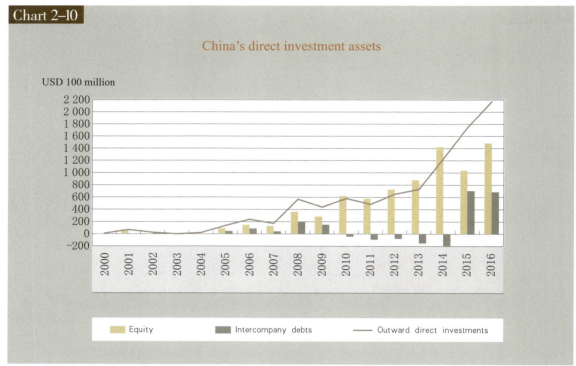

Chart 2-10

China's direct investment assets

USD 100 million

Equity   Intercompany debts   —— Outward direct investments

Source: SAFE.

the development of cooperation in international industrial capacity also helped the going–out of enterprises. However, the rapid growth of direct investments was also indicative of several issues that required attention. For instance, there were irrational outward investments in some fields, and some investments were characterized as "big affiliates with small parent companies" or "outward investments right after the establishment of domestic companies." Hence, it is necessary for domestic investors to guard against risks from overseas investments. In terms of the composition of investments, equity investment assets recorded a net increase of USD 148.4 billion; up by 43 percent and accounting for nearly 70 percent of the newly increased direct assets. The equity investments were long–term investments, and their rapid growth indicated that domestic enterprises were focusing on long–term investments. Loan assets to overseas affiliates recorded a net increase of USD 68.8 billion, down by 2 percent year on year. In particular, they recorded a net increase of USD 29.7 in Q1 and about USD 10 billion in the following three quarters respectively.

In terms of sectors, direct investment assets of the non–financial sector recorded a net increase of USD 193.8 billion, up by 32 percent year on year. The top five outward direct investment destinations were Hong Kong SAR, the Cayman Islands, the United States, the BVI, and Singapore, accounting for 93 percent of the total and reflecting that Chinese enterprises

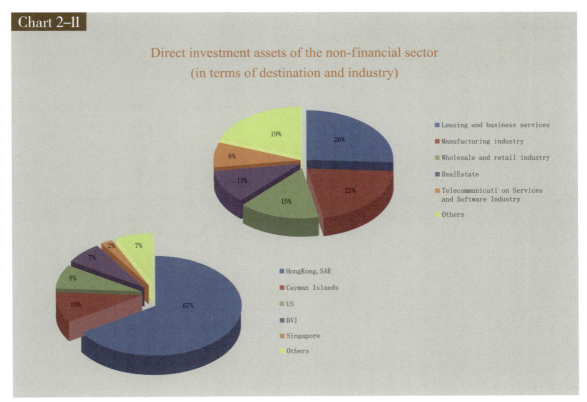

Chart 2-11

Direct investment assets of the non-financial sector
(in terms of destination and industry)

Source: SAFE.

focused on investing in countries and regions with fewer capital regulations. In terms of industries, leasing and business services, and manufacturing accounted for over 50 percent of the total (see Chart 2–11). The direct investment assets of the financial sector recorded a net increase of USD 21.9 billion, down by 22 percent, which was mainly contributed by banks, insurance companies, and other financial institutions.

Direct investment liabilities[①] **maintained a significant net inflow.** In 2016, direct investment liabilities recorded a net increase of USD 170.6 billion, down by 30 percent year on year.

In terms of the composition of the investments, equity investment liabilities recorded a net increase of USD 164.2 billion, down by 22 percent year on year (see Chart 2–12). Equity investments were still at a high level, reflecting that China was consistently attracting foreign capital inflows against the background of the uneven economic development. Loans from overseas affiliates posted a net decrease of USD 6.4 billion, down by 79 percent year on year. In particular, they recorded net reimbursements of USD 3.5 billion in Q1 but resumed the

① Direct investment liabilities are mainly composed of foreign direct investments. Reverse investments to domestic parent companies by overseas subsidiaries are also included.

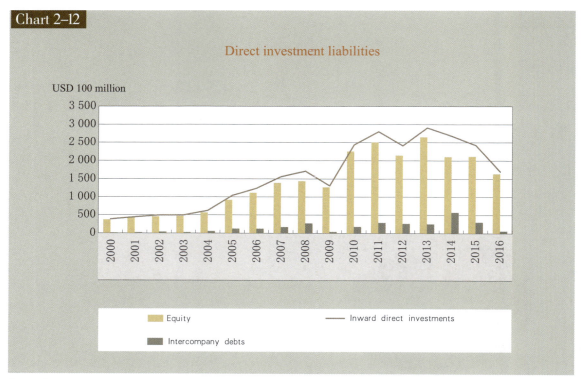

Chart 2-12

Direct investment liabilities

USD 100 million

Source: SAFE.

trend of inflows beginning in the second quarter. The deleveraging process of domestic entities came to an end and the demand for cross-border financing rebounded.

In terms of sectors, direct investment liabilities of the non-financial sector posted a net increase of USD 162.5 billion, up by 26 percent year on year and accounting for 95 percent of the total. In terms of industries, manufacturing was the most attractive industry for foreign direct investors, whose contribution rose by 8 percentage points. The contribution of leasing and business services dropped by 4 percentage points, and the contribution of information transmission and software and information technology services rose by 2 percentage points. The change reflected China's comparative advantage and competition in manufacturing and the information industry to attract capital inflows. The main source was still Hong Kong SAR, followed by Singapore and Taiwan PRC. Direct investment liabilities of the financial sector recorded a net inflow of USD 8.1 billion, down by 66 percent year on year. One reason was the capital withdrawals of some foreign strategic investments in domestic banks. Another reason was the drop in the profits of foreign-funded financial institutions, which caused a drop in the increase of cumulative profits.

Box 4

The Process and Characteristics of Overseas Investments by Chinese Enterprises

I. The going-abroad process of enterprises

Since the China's reform and opening, the going–abroad process of Chinese enterprises has experienced several phrases. In 2000, the going–abroad strategy was formally proposed at the Fifth Plenary Session of the Fifteenth Central Committee of the CPC. Thereafter, the Party Central Committee and the State Council successively put forward strategies to further enhance the degree of opening and to establish a new open economic regime.

Phase I(from 1980 to 1999): during the earlier period of reform and opening, the main strategy focused on attracting foreign investments. The volume of overseas direct investments (ODI) was small. **Phase II** (from 2000 to 2007): after 2000, overseas investments accelerated. According to the MOFCOM (the same below), ODI exceeded USD 10 billion and USD 20 billion in 2005 and 2006 respectively. **Phase III** (from 2008 to 2013): as external assets were undervalued as a result of the global financial crisis, China's overseas investments accelerated further. In 2008, ODI exceeded USD 50 billion for the first time in history. In 2013, ODI exceeded USD 100 billion. **Phase IV** (2014 to the present): the amount of ODI gradually came close to that of FDI and finally exceeded it.

II. The major characteristics of the going-abroad process for enterprises

A late start, rapid development, and great potential. In terms of flows, from 2003 to 2015 the ODI of the non–financial sectors grew by a yearly average of 33 percent. In terms of outstanding amounts, the ODI exceeded USD 1 trillion in 2015 for the first time in history. From 2003 to 2015, the outstanding amount of ODI rose by a yearly average of 30 percent. Until the end of 2014, the outstanding amount of ODI accounted for 7 percent of GDP. Compared with the 38 percent, 20 percent, and 47 percent in the United States, Japan, Germany, respectively, there was still a large gap.

The investment destinations were mainly located in Asia but they gradually expanded to the developing countries. In terms of flows, since 2007 China's direct investments to Asia have maintained high levels, totaling 70 percent of all ODI. In terms of the outstanding amounts, Asia, Europe, and Latin America accounted for 68 percent, 12 percent, and 8 percent respectively.

The trend of a sector change was obvious and the sector distribution was scattered. In terms of the flows, the mining sector accounted for 48 percent in 2003 but the ratio was reduced to 8 percent in 2015. The rental and services sector accounted for 10 percent in 2003 and the ratio rose to 25 percent in 2015 (see Chart 4–1). At the end of 2015, in terms of the outstanding amount, the rental and services sector accounted for 37 percent.

Chart C4–1

The sector distribution of China's ODI

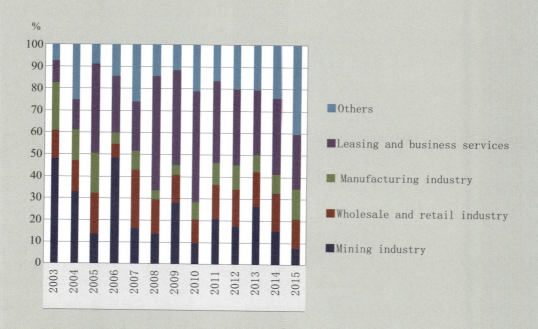

Source: Wind Database.

Privately–owned enterprises kept pace with state–owned enterprises. At the end of 2006, state–owned enterprises accounted for 81 percent of ODI, and non–state–owned enterprises accounted for 19 percent. At the end of 2015, state–owned enterprises and non–state–owned enterprises accounted for half and half, nearly equal to each other.

Overseas investments were cyclical with the prices of large commodities. From 2011 to

2012, the prices of large commodities reached their highest levels in history. Meanwhile, overseas acquisitions by Chinese enterprises in the energy and mining sector accounted for as much as 64 percent of the total overseas acquisitions of China's enterprises. Since 2016, as the prices of large commodities declined, overseas acquisitions in the energy and mining sector were reduced to 2 percent of total overseas acquisitions in that year.

Holding acquisitions dominated. In the first quarter of 2016, holding acquisitions reached USD 100.8 billion and accounted for 96 percent. Among the 10 largest deals, 9 deals were full acquisitions. Among 199 deals, 137 were holding acquisitions, accounting for 77 percent.

In general, the rapid growth of China's ODI is a result of the enhancement of its comprehensive national strength, improvements in the degree of opening, and the steady advancement of the Belt and Road proposal and international energy cooperation. ODI is helpful to boost economic growth and to realize mutual benefits and win–win results from joint development. But since 2016, some of the ODI of Chinese enterprises showed irrational trends and abnormal phenomena, thus requiring active guidance so as to maintain more healthy and orderly development. We have a very clear ODI strategy and management principle. We encourage enterprises to take part in international economic competition and cooperation so as to promote the transformation and updating of the domestic economy and to deepen mutually beneficial cooperation with other countries. By following the principles of "enterprises entities, market–oriented principles, international customs, and governmental guidance," we support capable and eligible enterprises to carry out authentic and regulated overseas investments.

(IV) Portfolio Investments

Net outflows of portfolio investments decreased. In 2016, portfolio investments recorded a net outflow of USD 62.2 billion, down by 6 percent year on year (see Chart 2–13). In particular, the first quarter posted a significant outflow, the second quarter recorded a net inflow, but the third quarter again recorded a net outflow, followed by the fourth quarter, in which the net outflow increased further. In terms of the composition of the investments, net outflows of equity investments decreased but net outflows of bond investments increased. In 2016, net outflows of equity investments totaled USD 19.6 billion, down by 21 percent, and net outflows of bond investments totaled USD 42.6 billion, up by 2 percent.

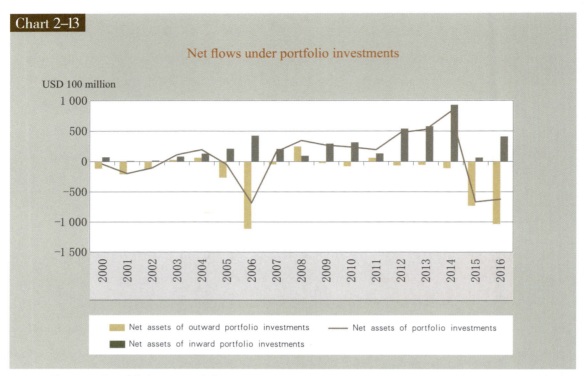

Chart 2–13

Net flows under portfolio investments

USD 100 million

Legend:
- Net assets of outward portfolio investments
- Net assets of inward portfolio investments
- Net assets of portfolio investments

Note: Positive outward portfolio investments indicate a decrease in outward investments in equities and bonds, and vice versa. Positive inward portfolio investments indicate an increase in inward investments in equities and bonds, and vice versa.
Source: SAFE.

Outward portfolio investments continued to post an increase in net outflows. In 2016, China's outward portfolio investments recorded a net outflow of USD 103.4 billion, up by 41 percent year on year. In particular, equity investments posted a net outflow of USD 38.5 billion, down by 3 percent. Bond investments recorded a net outflow of USD 64.9 billion, up by 93 percent.

In terms of the different channels, first, outward bond investments by financial institutions surged remarkably, posting a net outflow of USD 48.2 billion, up by 51 percent. Second, the opening up of the capital market led to increasing equity investments in both inward and outward directions. Net outflows under the Shanghai–Hong Kong connect (southbound) totaled USD 13.3 billion, up by 105 percent year on year (USD 27.3 billion in 2015).Third, net outflows of QDIIs and RQDIIs decreased. Outstanding equity and bond investments by QDIIs and RQFIIs totaled USD 5.7 billion, a decrease of USD 16.3 billion. Fourth, bonds issued by nonresidents in the domestic market and purchased by residents totaled USD 6 billion, which was four times that in 2015.

Inward portfolio investments increased significantly due to the opening up of the bond market. In 2016, inward portfolio investments recorded a net inflow of USD 41.2 billion, up by 512 percent. With the exception of the first quarter, which recorded a net outflow of USD 18.9 billion, the other three quarters all recorded a net inflow. In particular, inward equity investments recorded a net inflow of USD 18.9 billion, up by USD 27 billion. Inward bond investments recorded a net inflow of USD 22.3 billion, whereas in 2015 theyhad recorded a net outflow of USD 8.2 billion. The change in bond investmentsfrom outflows to inflows was the main reason for the increase in portfolio investments. In 2016, China further opened its inter-bank bond market to foreign investors and reformed the QFII and RQFII foreign-exchange policy by increasing the upper-limit quota and facilitating capital flows, which together increased capital-inflow channels.

In terms of the major channels, first, investments by foreign investors in the domestic bond market amounted to USD 37 billion, an increase of USD 28.1 billion year on year. Second, stocks and bonds issued by Chinese institutions in offshore markets and purchased by nonresidents decreased from USD 35.7 billion in 2015 to USD 25.6 billion in 2016. Third, capital inflows via the Shanghai-Hong Kong connect (northbound) and the Shenzhen-Hong Kong connect (northbound) increased from USD 3 billion in 2015 to USD 6.9 billion in 2016. Fourth, the decline in outstanding bankers' acceptances with drafts[1] was the main driver for the increase in net outflows, which increased from USD 8.5 billion in 2015 to USD 28.3 billion in 2016.

(V) Other Investments

Net outflows of other investments declined. In 2016, other investments posted a net outflow of USD 303.5 billion, down by 30 percent year on year (see Chart 2-14). Net outflows of major items under other investments all decelerated. In particular, net assets of currency and deposits, loans, and trade credits increased by USD 33.3 billion, USD 134.3 billion, and USD 84.6 billion respectively, down by 81 percent, 37 percent, and 22 percent.

Capital outflows under other investments continued to increase. In 2016, outward other investments recorded a net increase of USD 333.6 billion, up by 305 percent year on year. Domestic entities were more actively involved in international activities. Loans, trade credits, other assets, and currency and deposits increased by USD 114.7 billion, USD 100.8 billion, USD 74.3 billion, and USD 43.5 billion respectively year on year.

---

[1] According to *Balance of Payments and International Investment Position Manual, Sixth Edition*, bankers' acceptances with drafts are moved from the category of other investments/loans to the category of portfolio investments/debt securities.

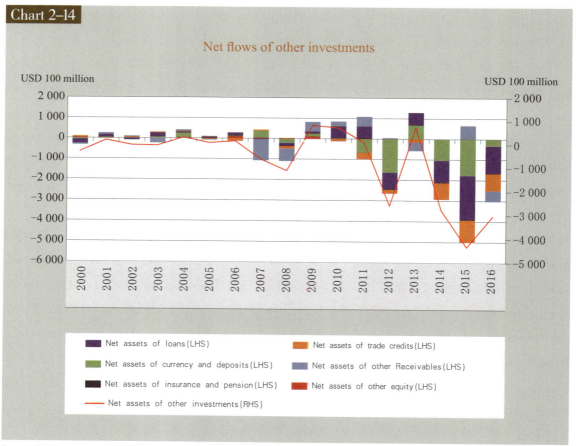

Chart 2–14

Net flows of other investments

USD 100 million

USD 100 million

Legend:
- Net assets of loans (LHS)
- Net assets of trade credits (LHS)
- Net assets of currency and deposits (LHS)
- Net assets of other Receivables (LHS)
- Net assets of insurance and pension (LHS)
- Net assets of other equity (LHS)
- Net assets of other investments (RHS)

Source: SAFE.

External liabilities under other investments changed from inflows to outflows. In 2016, other investment liabilities recorded a net inflow of USD 30.1 billion, whereas in 2015 they recorded a net outflow of USD 351.5 billion. On the one hand, the net outflow of external loans amounted to USD 19.6 billion, down by 88 percent year on year. After a period of external debt deleveraging and the launch of comprehensive macro prudential regulation on cross–border financing, external debts borrowed by domestic enterprises rebounded and beginning in the second quarter external loans posted a net inflow for consecutive three quarters. On the other hand, net inflows of currency and deposits decreased by USD 47.7 billion, 51 percent less than the decrease in 2015. In addition, trade credit liabilities increased by USD 16.2 billion (that is, the increase in payables and advances under trade credit), whereas in 2015 they recorded a decrease of USD 62.3 billion. Other liabilities increased by USD 23.9 billion, mainly due to the China's increased subscription share in the IMF, which means the IMF's increased claims to the PBOC.

Different Trade Credit Instruments by Enterprises

In August 2016, the new edition of the rules for trade credit investigations was launched and sample enterprises reported their data for July. Compared with the old edition, the method changed from stratified sampling to the sampling of enterprises above a designated size. The statistical coverage was adjusted as well. Sample enterprises should report their comprehensive trade payables and collectables and no longer differentiate between bank financing and enterprise credits.[①] According to the report of sample enterprises, different types of sample enterprises used different trade credit instruments.

The manufacturing and wholesale and retail industries ranked as the top two industries with respect to outstanding trade credit with distinguishing characteristics. Manufacturing and wholesale and retail enterprises accounted for 95 percent of total receivables, 93 percent of payables, 84 percent of advance receipts, and 66 percent of advance payments. They were the major contributors to trade credits, especially electronic equipment manufacturing, which accounted for over 50 percent of total receivables and total payables. Transportation manufacturing and air transportation were special, and they accounted for 23 percent of total export advance receipts and 32 percent of total import advance payments, far higher than their contribution to exports and imports (2 percent and 1 percent respectively).

Foreign enterprises were more active than Chinese-funded enterprises in trade credit financing to avoid foreign-exchange risks by financing operations. 57 percent of total export receivables and 43 percent of import advance payments were contributed by foreign–funded enterprises, although they accounted for 60 percent of total exports and 52 percent of total imports. In terms of monthly data, the contribution of foreign–funded enterprises to export receivables increased from 52 percent in July to 57 percent in November and this was the main source of export receivables. However, foreign–funded enterprises accounted for 62 percent of total import payables, 10 percentage points higher than the contribution of foreign–funded enterprises to imports. When circumstances

---

① Data in Box 5 are derived from the trade credit investigation from July to November of 2016, and the trade credit data are the comprehensive trade credit data reported by the sample enterprises, that is to say, both the trade credits of enterprises and the trade financing of banks.

related to the exchange rate or the interest rate changed, foreign–funded enterprises took advantage of cross–border capital allocations by creating more receivables and allocating more capital overseas for profits.

Large enterprises were more capable in terms of utilizing trade credits, and the concentration of advance receipts and payments was higher than the concentration of receivables and payables. The contributions of the top 10 and top 100 sample enterprises to receivables, advance receipts, payables, and advance payments were far higher than their contributions to exports and imports. Moreover, the top 100 enterprises accounted for 75 percent of export advance receipts and 96 percent of import advance payments whereas they contributed only 6 percent of the exports and 12 percent of the imports. Among the top 100 enterprises for export receivables and import payables, 61 and 46 respectively were from the electronic equipment manufacturing industry.

Nearly 60 percent of export receivables and import payables were trade credits with affiliates, especially among large enterprises, foreign-funded enterprises, and manufacturing enterprises. First, 57 percent of total export receivables and 55 percent of total import payables were with affiliates, whereas only 10 percent of total export advance receipts and 16 percent of total import advance payments were with affiliates. It was a common arrangement for affiliates to finance via receivables and payables. Second, affiliate transactions were popular in large enterprises. For the top ten enterprises for export receivables and import payables, their outstanding with affiliates accounted for 81 percent and 82 percent of the total respectively. Third, 79 percent of the receivables of foreign–funded enterprises and 68 percent of their payables were with their parent companies or affiliates. Fourth, manufacturing enterprises were more actively involved with their affiliates with respect to receivables and payables. In particular, for electronic equipment enterprises, receivables and payables with their affiliates accounted for 81 percent and 66 percent of the total respectively.

III. International Investment Position

China's external assets, liabilities,① and net assets were all on the rise. At end–December 2016, China's external financial assets and liabilities reached USD 6 466.6 billion and USD 4 666 billion respectively, a year–on–year increase of 5 percent and 4 percent respectively. Net assets reached USD 1 800.5 billion, an increase of 8 percent and equivalent to USD 127.7 billion (see Chart 3–1).

For the first time, the ratio of private-sector holdings of external assets accounted for more than one-half of the total assets. Among the external financial assets, at end–December 2016 outward direct investments amounted to USD 1 317.2 billion, a year–on–year increase of 20 percent. The investments reached a historical high of 20 percent of total assets, 3 percentage points more than that at end–December 2015. Portfolio investments amounted

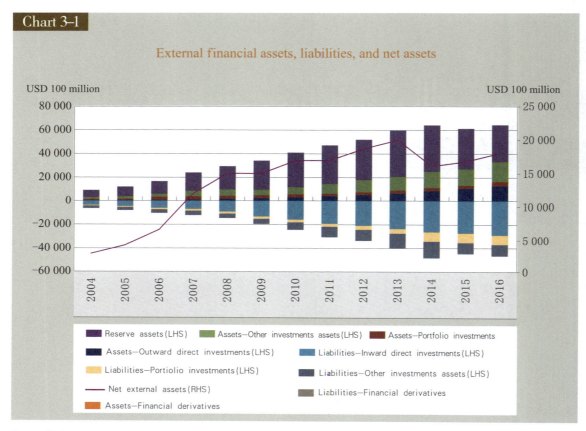

Chart 3–1

External financial assets, liabilities, and net assets

Source: SAFE.

① External financial assets and liabilities include direct investments, portfolio investments, and other investments, such as loans and deposits. Outward direct investments are included as financial assets because the equities issued by nonresident direct investment enterprises and held by domestic investors are the same type of financial instruments as the equity investments in portfolio investments. The difference is that direct investments require a higher threshold of equity holdings so as to reflect a significant influence or control over the production and operations of the enterprises. Inward direct investments belong to external financial liabilities because foreign investors hold equities in foreign–owned companies.

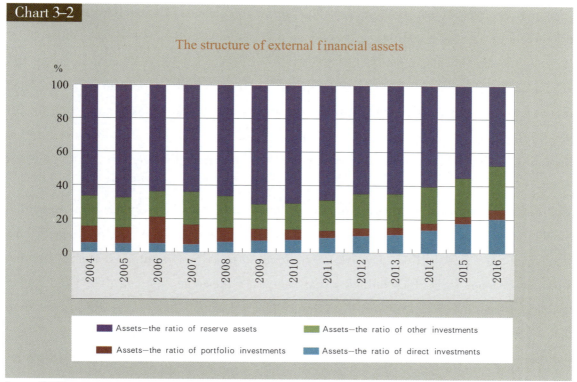

Chart 3–2

The structure of external financial assets

Assets—the ratio of reserve assets
Assets—the ratio of other investments
Assets—the ratio of portfolio investments
Assets—the ratio of direct investments

Source: SAFE.

to USD 365.1 billion, a year–on–year increase of 40 percent and accounting for 6 percent of external assets, 1 percentage point more than that at end–December 2015. Other investments, such as loans and deposits, amounted to USD 1 681.1 billion, a year–on–year increase of 21 percent and accounting for 26 percent of external assets, 3 percentage points more than that at end–December 2015. International reserves amounted to USD 3 097.8 billion, a year–on–year decline of 9 percent. Among the international reserves, foreign–exchange reserves amounted to USD 3 010.5 billion, a year–on–year decline of 10 percent. As the largest component, international reserves accounted for 48 percent of external assets, 7 percentage points less than that at end–December 2015 and a historical low since China's first IIP statement at end–December 2004 (see Chart 3–2).

The increase in foreign direct investments and the restoration of other foreign investments contributed to the increase in external liabilities. Among the external liabilities, foreign direct investments amounted to USD 2 865.9 billion at end–December 2016,[①] a year–on–

---

① The inward foreign direct investment position includes FDI stocks of both the non–financial sector and the financial sector. The position includes inter–company lending as well as other debt positions among the relevant offices. The statistics also reflect the impact of revaluations. The statistical coverage of inward FDI is different from the cumulative statistics of the Ministry of Commerce. Over the years, the latter used the cumulative FDI equity investment flows as the inward FDI position.

year increase of 6 percent. Continuing as the largest component, FDI liabilities accounted for 61 percent of external liabilities, 1 percentage point more than that at end–December 2015. Portfolio investments amounted to USD 808.6 billion, a year–on–year decline of 1 percent and accounting for 17 percent of external liabilities. The ratio was 1 percentage point less than that at end–December 2015. Other investments such as loans and deposits amounted to USD 984.9 billion, a year–on–year increase of 2 percent and accounting for 21 percent of external liabilities, a slight decline of 0.4 percentage point from that at end–December 2015 (see Chart 3–3).

The deficit in investment income declined. In 2016, China's investment income recorded a deficit of USD 65 billion, a year–on–year decline of 6 percent. Revenue from investments reached USD 198.4 billion, a year–on–year increase of 6 percent. Investment income payments reached USD 263.4 billion, a year–on–year increase of 2 percent. The yield spread between assets and liabilities was –2.6 percentage points, 0.1 percentage point more than that in 2015 (see Chart 3–4). In the long run, the structure of external financial assets and liabilities will determine the deficit in the investment income account. At end–December 2016, the largest component in external assets was reserve assets, which were invested in

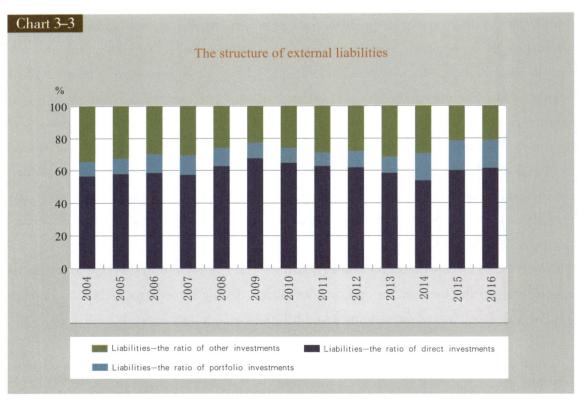

Chart 3–3

The structure of external liabilities

Legend:
- Liabilities—the ratio of other investments
- Liabilities—the ratio of direct investments
- Liabilities—the ratio of portfolio investments

Source: SAFE.

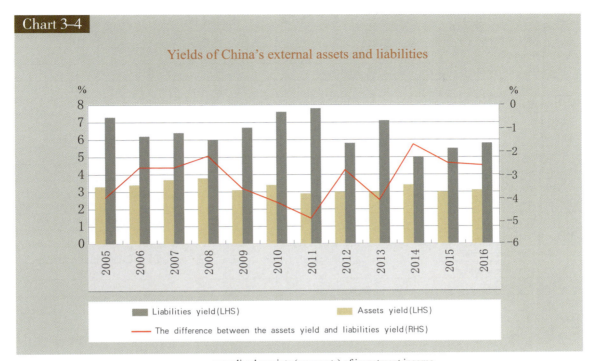

Chart 3–4

Yields of China's external assets and liabilities

Note: 1. Yields on assets (liabilities)= $\dfrac{\text{annualized receipts (payments) of investment income}}{(\text{positions at the reference year-end+positions at the previous year-end})/2}$

2. The difference between the yields of assets and liabilities= the yields of assets – the yields of liabilities
Source: SAFE.

assets with higher liquidity and lower yields than other types of investments such as direct investments. As a result, the annual yields of China's external assets from 2005 to 2016 were 3.3 percent. Amongexternal liabilities, inward FDI was the major component. As long–term and stable investments, equity liabilities in inward FDI require a higher yield than other types of investments. From 2005 to 2016, the average annual yields of inward investments were 6.4 percent.

Table 3-1 China's international investment position at end-December 2016   Unit：USD 100 million

Items	Line No.	2016
Net International Investment Position [①]	1	18 005
Assets	2	64 666
1 Direct investment	3	13 172
1.1 Equity and investment fund shares	4	10 650
1.2 Debt instruments	5	2 522
2 Portfolio investment	6	3 651

① Net Internartion Investment position means assets minus liabilities, "+" means net assets, "–" means net liabilities The Chant is Counted by rounding principle.

Items	Line No.	2016
2.1 Equity and investment fund shares	7	2 149
2.2 Debt securities	8	1 502
3 Financial derivatives (other than reserves) and employee stock options	9	52
4 Other investment	10	16 811
4.1 Other equity	11	1
4.2 Currency and deposits	12	3 816
4.3 Loans	13	5 622
4.4 Insurance, pension, and standardized guarantee schemes	14	123
4.5 Trade credit and advances	15	6 145
4.6 Other accounts receivable	16	1 105
5 Reserve assets	17	30 978
5.1 Monetary gold	18	679
5.2 Special drawing rights	19	97
5.3 Reserve position in the IMF	20	96
5.4 Foreign currency reserves	21	30 105
5.5 Other reserve assets	22	2
Liabilities	23	46 660
1 Direct investment	24	28 659
1.1 Equity and investment fund shares	25	26 543
1.2 Debt instruments	26	2 117
2 Portfolio investment	27	8 086
2.1 Equity and investment fund shares	28	5 927
2.2 Debt securities	29	2 159
3 Financial derivatives (other than reserves) and employee stock options	30	66
4 Other investment	31	9 849
4.1 Other equity	32	0
4.2 Currency and deposits	33	3 156
4.3 Loans	34	3 236
4.4 Insurance, pension, and standardized guarantee schemes	35	88
4.5 Trade credit and advances	36	2 883
4.6 Other accounts payable	37	391
4.7 Special drawing rights	38	94

Source: SAFE.

Box 6

External Assets and Liabilities in China's Banking Sector

At end–December 2016, external assets and liabilities of China's banking sector increased and net liabilities declined. External assets reached USD 877.6 billion,[1] a year–on–year

[1] The data are derived from the *Statistical Report on External Assets and Liabilities*, a statistical reporting requirement of the SAFE. At end–December 2015, China participated in the international banking statistics of the Bank for International Settlements and began to report cross–border financial assets and liabilities of Chinese banks on a quarterly basis. The box is based on data reported at end–December 2016.

increase of 19 percent and accounting for 14 percent of China's external assets.[①] The external liabilities of China's banking sector reached USD 964.5 billion, a year–on–year increase of 2 percent and accounting for 21 percent of China's external liabilities. The net liability positions were USD 86.9 billion, a year–on–year decline of 59 percent.

Among the external financial assets, loans and deposits accounted for approximately 80 percent of the outstanding claims. Debt securities accounted for a small portion but were growing at a high rate. Other investments increased due to the increase in equity investments in overseas subsidiaries. Cross–border loan and deposit assets held by China's banking sector amounted to USD 670.5 billion, a year–on–year increase of 16 percent and accounting for 76 percent of the banks' external assets. Among them, loan assets dominated. Cross–border portfolio investments amounted to USD 95.2 billion, a year–on–year increase of 50 percent and accounting for 11 percent of external assets. The rise was due to increasing investments in debt securities in the US and Hong Kong SAR markets. Other investments, such as financial derivatives and equity investments amounted to USD 111.9 billion, an increase of 12 percent and accounting for 13 percent of external assets. Equity investments in overseas subsidiaries were the major contributor.

Among external liabilities, more than half were loans and deposits. The portion of debt securities declined, whereas the portion of other investments increased due to surging IPOs abroad. The loan and deposit liabilities of China's banking sector amounted to USD 501.1 billion, a year–on–year increase of 3 percent and accounting for 52 percent of the banks' external liabilities. Among them, loans borrowed from related banks werea major component. Debt securities amounted to USD 116.9 billion, a decline of 16 percent and accounting for 12 percent of external liabilities. The decline was due to repayments of acceptances of letters of credit by trade–related banks. Other investments such as financial derivatives and equity liabilities amounted to USD 346.4 billion, a year–on–year increase of 8 percent and accounting for 36 percent of external liabilities. Domestic banks, such as the Postal Savings Bank of China, were listed on the Hong Kong SAR share market, contributing to the increase in cross–border equity liabilities (see Chart C6–1).

In terms of currency, China's banking sector recorded net foreign-exchange external assets and net RMB liabilities. At end–December 2016, cross–border

---

① The positions of external assets include international reserve assets. If the international reserve assets are excluded, the external assets of the banks constitute 26 percent of China's total external assets.

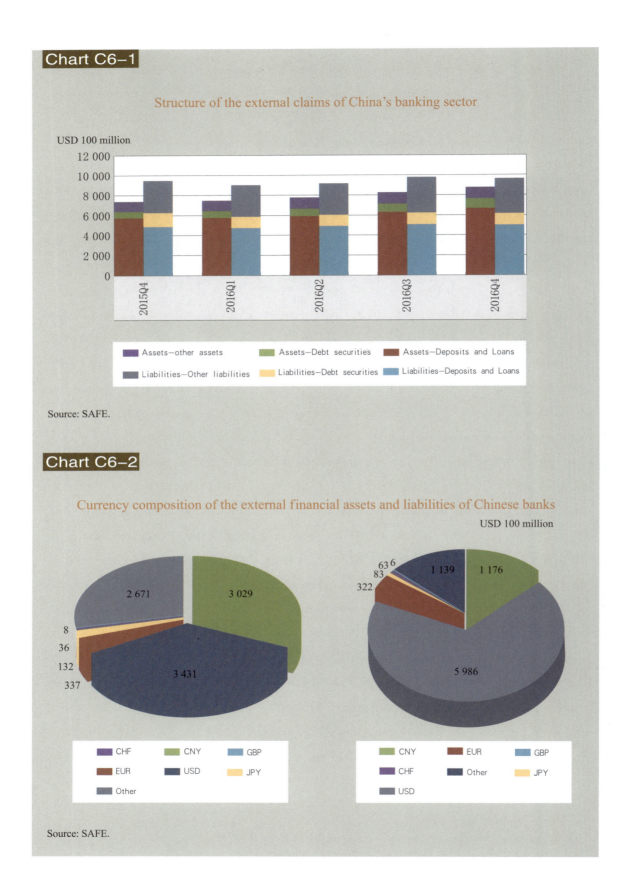

Chart C6-1

Structure of the external claims of China's banking sector

USD 100 million

Legend:
- Assets—other assets
- Assets—Debt securities
- Assets—Deposits and Loans
- Liabilities—Other liabilities
- Liabilities—Debt securities
- Liabilities—Deposits and Loans

(Categories: 2015Q4, 2016Q1, 2016Q2, 2016Q3, 2016Q4)

Source: SAFE.

Chart C6-2

Currency composition of the external financial assets and liabilities of Chinese banks

USD 100 million

Left pie: 3 029; 3 431; 2 671; 8; 36; 132; 337
Legend: CHF, CNY, GBP, EUR, USD, JPY, Other

Right pie: 1 176; 1 139; 6; 63; 83; 322; 5 986
Legend: CNY, EUR, GBP, CHF, Other, JPY, USD

Source: SAFE.

USD assets amounted to USD 598.6 billion, a year–on–year increase of 11 percent and accounting for 68 percent of the banks' external assets. The expansion in USD loans and debt security investments was a major contributor. RMB assets amounted to USD 117.6 billion, twice the amount at end–December 2015, 13 percent of the external assets. Cross–border loans played a major role. External assets in other foreign currencies amounted to USD 161.4 billion, 19 percent of the external assets. USD liabilities amounted to USD 343.1 billion, an increase of 47 percent and accounting for 36 percent of external liabilities. RMB liabilities amounted to USD 302.9 billion, a decline of 31 percent and accounting for 31 percent of external liabilities. External liabilities in other foreign currencies amounted to USD 318.4 billion and accounted for 33 percent. In terms of net assets and liabilities, Chinese banks recorded net liabilities of USD 185.3 billion in RMB and net assets of USD 98.4 billion in foreign currencies, a decline of 51 percent and 42 percent from the net positions at end–December 2015 respectively.

In terms of the counter-party country/region of the external positions, the advanced economies and the off-shore centers were major counter-parties. The top 3 debtor economies of Chinese bank investments were: Hong Kong SAR (USD 224.4 billion), the US (USD 113.1 billion), and Singapore (USD 34.5 billion). They received 26 percent, 13 percent, and 4 percent of Chinese bank investments respectively. The top 3 creditor economies of the external liabilities of Chinese banks were: Hong Kong SAR (USD 524.2 billion), Taiwan PRC (USD 59.8 billion), and Japan (USD 36.8 billion). They contributed 54 percent, 6 percent, and 4 percent of the banks' total liabilities respectively.

Table C6-1 The structure of external assets and liabilities of China's banking sector at end-December 2016

Unit: 100 million of USD

		Assets		Liabilities		Net Assets
		Value	Ratio	Value	Ratio	Value
By instrument	Loans and deposits	6 705	76%	5 011	52%	1 694
	Debt securities	952	11%	1 169	12%	-218
	Other investments	1 119	13%	3 464	36%	-2 345
By currency	CNY	1 176	13%	3 029	31%	-1 853
	USD	5 986	68%	3 431	36%	2 555
	EUR	322	4%	337	3%	-15
	JPY	83	1%	132	1%	-49
	GBP	63	1%	36	0.4%	27
	Other	1 145	13%	2 680	28%	-1 534
Total		8 776	100%	9 645	100%	-869

Source: SAFE.

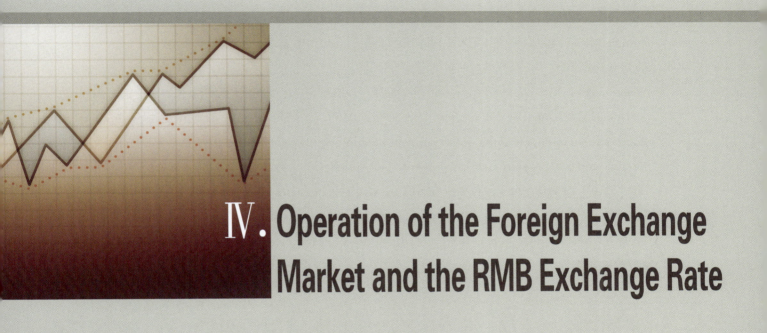

IV. Operation of the Foreign Exchange Market and the RMB Exchange Rate

(I) Trends in the RMB Exchange Rate

The RMB exchange rate against the major currencies showed both appreciations and depreciations. At the end of 2016, the mid-price of the RMB exchange rate against the USD was 6.9370, a depreciation of 6.4 percent from the end of 2015.The RMB spot exchange rate against the USD in the inter-bank foreign-exchange market (CNY) and in the offshore market (CNH)depreciated by 6.5 percent and 5.8 percent respectively (see Chart 4-1). The daily average spread between the CNH and the CNY was 134 bps (see Chart 4-2), lower than the 213 bps in 2015.

At the end of 2016,the mid-price of the RMB exchange rate against the EUR,100JPY, GBP, AUD, and CAD stood at 7.3068,5.9591,8.5094,5.0157, and 5.1406 respectively, a depreciation of 2.9 percent, a depreciation of 9.6 percent, an appreciation of 13 percent, a depreciation of 5.7 percent ,and a depreciation of 8.9 percent respectively.

The RMB exchange rate depreciated slightly against the basket of currencies. According to CFETS data, at the end of 2016 the RMB exchange-rate indexes of the CFETS, the BIS basket of currencies, and the SDR basket of currencies were 94.83, 96.24, and 95.50

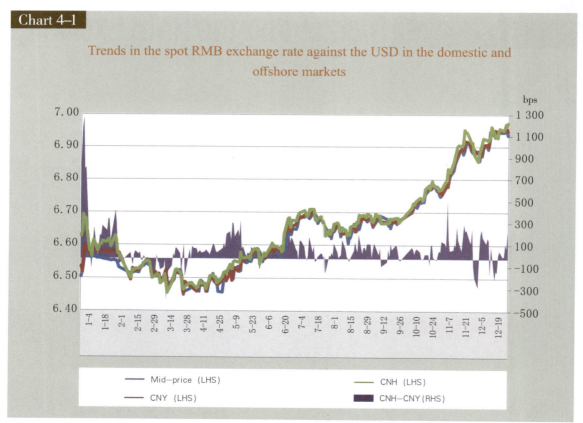

Chart 4-1

Trends in the spot RMB exchange rate against the USD in the domestic and offshore markets

Sources: CFETS, Reuters.

Chart 4–2

Spread of the spot RMB exchange rates against the USD in the domestic and offshore markets

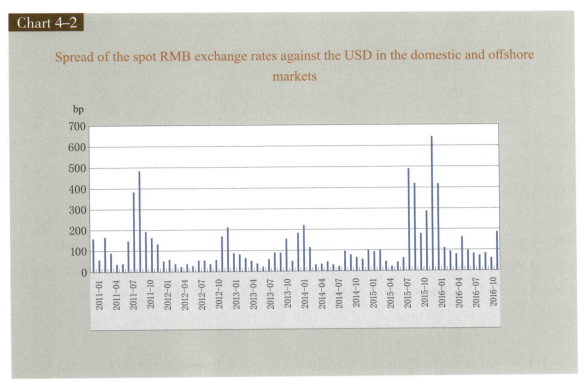

Note: The absolute values of the average daily spread.
Sources: CFETS, Reuters.

Chart 4–3

Trends in the effective RMB exchange rate

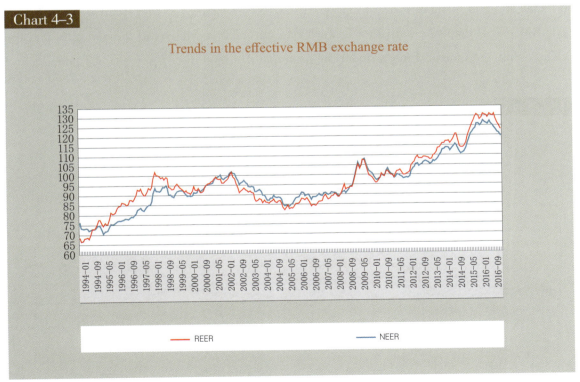

Source: BIS.

respectively, a depreciation of 6.1 percent, 5.4 percent, and 3.4 percent respectively from the end of the previous year.

According to the BIS, the nominal effective exchange rate of the RMB depreciated by 5.8 percent in 2016. Deducting for inflation, the real effective exchange rate of the RMB depreciated by 5.7 percent (see Chart 4–3). Since the exchange–rate regime reform in 2005, the nominal and real effective exchange rates of the RMB appreciated by37.3 percent and 47.1 percent respectively.

Expectations regarding the RMB exchange rate were basically stable. At the end of 2016, the one–year historical volatilities of the RMB exchange rate in the domestic and offshore markets stood at 2.7 percent and 3.4 percent, down by 12.3 percent and 21.4 percent from the end of 2015 respectively. The implied volatilities in the domestic and offshore options markets reached 5.2 percent and 8.1 percent, up by 2.9 percent and 8.7 percent from the end of 2015 respectively (see Chart 4–4). The RMB exchange rate was basically stable in terms of its two–directional fluctuations.

The RMB was weakened in the foreign-exchange forward market. Impacted by the interest–rate spread of domestic and foreign currencies, supply and demand in the foreign–exchange market, and market expectations, the RMB exhibited volatility and was weakened in the domestic and offshore forward markets in 2016 (see Chart 4–5 and Chart 4–6).The one–year RMB/USD domestic delivered forward rate, the offshore delivered forward rate, and the offshore delivered forward rate without the principal declined by 5.7 percent, 7.3 percent, and

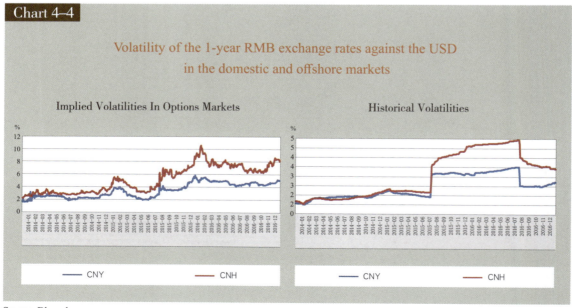

Chart 4–4

Volatility of the 1-year RMB exchange rates against the USD in the domestic and offshore markets

Source: Bloomberg.

Chart 4–5

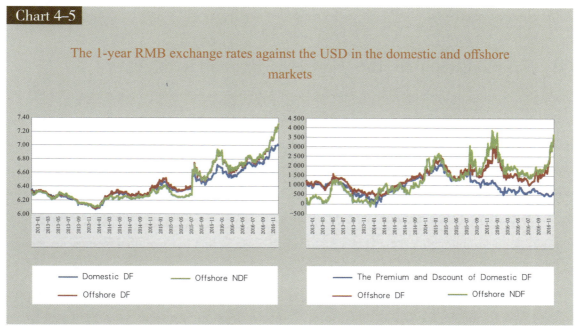

The 1-year RMB exchange rates against the USD in the domestic and offshore markets

Sources: CFETS, Reuters.

Chart 4–6

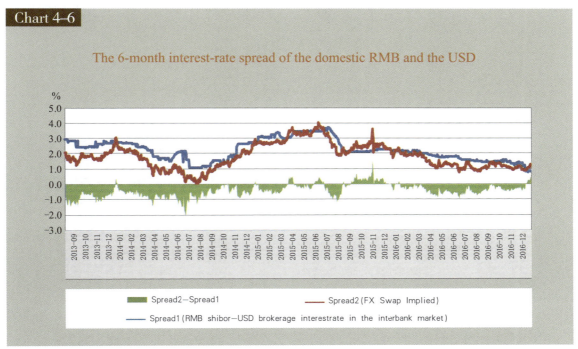

The 6-month interest-rate spread of the domestic RMB and the USD

Sources: CFETS, Reuters.

7.3 percent respectively.

(II) Transactions in the Foreign-Exchange Market

In 2016, the cumulative trading volume of the RMB/foreign-currency market totaled USD 20 trillion, an increase of 14 percent from the previous year (see Chart 4–7), with a daily average trading volume of USD 83.2 billion. The total trading volumes in the client market and the inter-bank market were USD 3 trillion and USD 17 trillion respectively.[①] Spot and derivative transactions saw a trading volume of USD 9 trillion and USD 11 trillion respectively (see Table 4–1). Derivatives, at 56 percent, accounted for a historical high share of the total transactions in the foreign-exchange market. This structure was close to that of the global foreign-exchange market (see Chart 4–8).

Growth of foreign-exchange spot transactions. In 2016, the spot foreign-exchange market saw a trading volume of USD9 trillion, up by 7 percent from the previous year. Spot purchases and sales of foreign exchange in the client market totaled USD 2.9 trillion (including banks, but excluding implementation of forwards), down by14 percent from the previous year. The spot

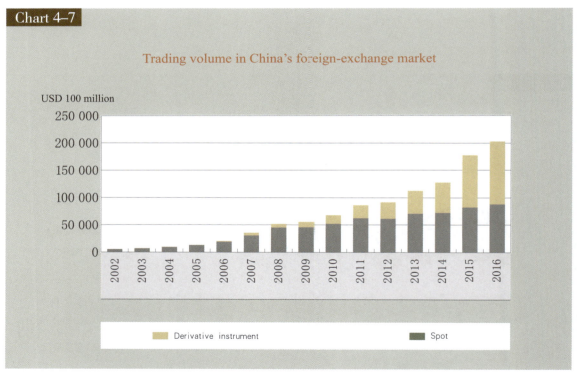

Chart 4–7

Trading volume in China's foreign-exchange market

Sources: SAFE, CFETS.

---

① The amount of transactions in the client market is the total amount of transactions including purchases and sales of foreign exchange by clients. The amount of transactions in the inter-bank market is the amount of unilateral transactions. The same as below.

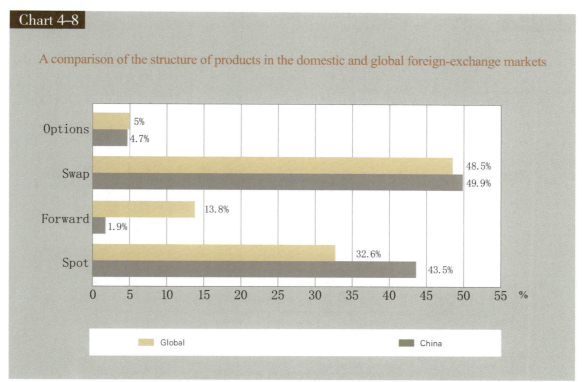

Chart 4–8

A comparison of the structure of products in the domestic and global foreign-exchange markets

Options: 5% (Global), 4.7% (China)
Swap: 48.5% (Global), 49.9% (China)
Forward: 13.8% (Global), 1.9% (China)
Spot: 32.6% (Global), 43.5% (China)

Global ▮ China ▮

Note: The data for China are from 2016; the global data are from a survey conducted by the BIS in April 2016.
Sources: SAFE, CFETS, BIS.

inter−bank foreign−exchange market saw a trading volume of USD 6 trillion, up by 22 percent from the previous year. The share of USD transactions was 97 percent.

A decrease in foreign-exchange forward transactions. In 2016, the forwards market saw a trading volume of USD 378.3 billion, down by 24 percent from the previous year. In the client market, purchases and sales of forwards in foreign exchange totaled USD 225.4billion, down by 51 percent from the previous year. Purchases and sales of forwards were USD 70.3 billion and USD 155.1 billion; down by 47 percent and 52 percent respectively (see Chart 4−9). Short− term 6−month transactions accounted for 59 percent of the total transactions, down by 11.4 percent from 2015. In the inter−bank foreign−exchange market, forwards totaled USD 152.9 billion, up 3.1 times from the previous year.

An increase in swap transactions. In 2016, cumulative foreign−exchange and currency swap transactions totaled USD 10 trillion, up by 18 percent from the previous year. Cumulative foreign−exchange and currency swap transactions in the client market reached USD 106.8 billion, down by 56 percent from the previous year. Spot purchases/forward sales and spot sales/forward purchases stood at USD 73.6 billion and USD 33.1 billion respectively, up by 2.5 times and down by 85 percent from the previous year respectively. This mainly reflected

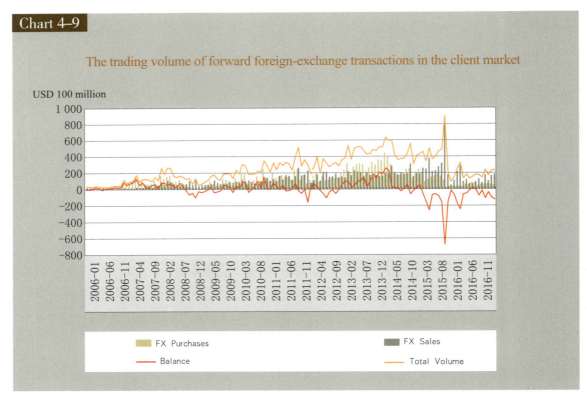

Chart 4–9

The trading volume of forward foreign-exchange transactions in the client market

USD 100 million

Legend: FX Purchases   FX Sales   Balance   Total Volume

Source: SAFE.

the impact of the large decline in the USD premium of forwards in enterprise transactions. The cumulative foreign–exchange and currency swap transactions in the inter–bank market reached USD 10 trillion, up by 20 percent from the previous year.

An increase in option transactions. In 2016, the trading volume of options totaled USD 955 billion, up by 1.4 times from the previous year. This shows that against the background of the two–directional fluctuations in the RMB exchange rate, options have a more obvious flexibility and attraction when managing exchange–rate risks. The client market saw a total trading volume of USD 207.9 billion, up by 79 percent from the previous year. The inter–bank market saw a total trading volume of USD 747.1 billion, up by 1.6 times from the previous year.

Foreign-exchange market participants remained basically stable. Proprietary transactions by banks continued to dominate (see Chart4–10). The share of inter–bank transactions among all foreign–exchange transactions rose from 75.4 percent in 2015 to 82 percent in 2016.The share of bank transactions with non–financial customers fell from 23 percent to 17 percent. The share of non–banking financial institutions was 0.8 percent, down by 0.7 percent.

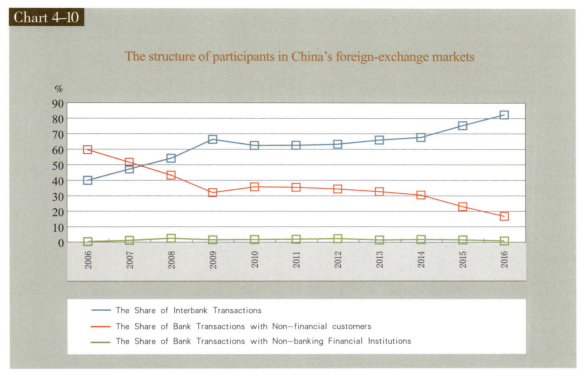

Chart 4–10

The structure of participants in China's foreign-exchange markets

— The Share of Interbank Transactions
— The Share of Bank Transactions with Non−financial customers
— The Share of Bank Transactions with Non−banking Financial Institutions

Sources: SAFE, CFETS.

Table 4-1   Transactions in the RMB/foreign-exchange market, 2016

Products	Trading Volume (100 million USD)
Spot	88 354
Client Market	29 085
Interbank Foreign Exchange Market	59 269
Forward	3 783
Client Market	2 254
Less than 3 months (including 3 months)	895
3 months to 1 year (including 1 year)	1 154
More than 1 year	205
Interbank Foreign Exchange Market	1 529
Less than 3 months (including 3 months)	1 195
3 months to 1 year (including 1 year)	305
More than 1 year	28
Foreign Exchange and Currency Swaps	101 297
Client Market	1 068

Products	Trading Volume (100 million USD)
Interbank Foreign Exchange Market	100 229
Less than 3 months (including 3 months)	88 520
3 months to 1 year (including 1 year)	11 592
More than 1 year	117
Options	9 550
Client Market	2 079
Foreign Exchange Call Options/RMB Put Options	1 021
Foreign Exchange Put Options/RMB Call Options	1 058
Less than 3 months (including 3 months)	668
3 months to 1 year (including 1 year)	1 196
More than 1 year	215
Interbank Foreign Exchange Market	7 471
Less than 3 months (including 3 months)	6 998
3 months to 1 year (including 1 year)	468
More than 1 year	4
Total	202 984
Client Market	34 486
Interbank Foreign Exchange Market	168 498
Including: Spots	88 354
Forwards	3 783
Foreign Exchange and Currency Swaps	101 297
Options	9 550

Note: The trading volumes here are all unilateral transactions and the data employ rounded-off numbers.
Sources: SAFE, CFETS.

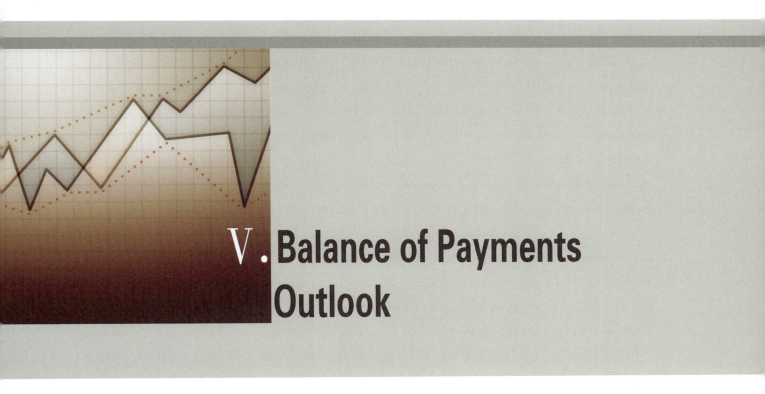

V. Balance of Payments Outlook

In 2017, China's balance of payments will continue to record a surplus in the current account and a deficit in the capital and financial account (excluding reserve assets). Cross–border capital flows will continue to converge to a balanced state.

The current account will maintain a reasonable surplus. First, the surplus in the trade in goods account will remain. In term of exports, although trade frictions pose potential risks for China's exports, the global economy will stabilize in 2017, contributing to a stable external demand for Chinese goods. According to the IMF's latest forecast, the global economy will grow at 3.4 percent in 2017, 0.3 percentage point more than that in 2016. The advanced economies will grow at 0.3 percentage point more than that in 2016, and the emerging market economies and the developing countries will grow at 0.4 percentage point more than that in 2016. In the meantime, stable progress in The Belt and Road initiative will benefit exports for countries in that region. In term of imports, demand for imports will be stable due to the performance of the domestic economy, and international commodity markets will continue to recover, contributing to stable Chinese imports. Second, the deficit in trade in services will grow steadily. As a major deficit item in trade in services, travel will record a stable deficit, as demand for travel and study abroad will progressively stabilize. The structural adjustments will affect receipts and payments of enterprise services, helping to narrow the deficits in services other than travel. Moreover, as investment assets, such as outward direct investments by the private sector, expand, revenue from these investments will grow. As a result, in 2017 the ratio of the current account surplus to GDP will be within the globally recognized reasonable range.

The capital and financial account will record a smaller deficit. On the one hand, the unstable and uncertain international environment may contribute to shifting market sentiment, triggering fluctuations in China's capital flows. Unclear political and economic events, such as adjustments in US policies under the Trump administration, negotiations on Brexit, and voting in the major European countries, may pose challenges to economic globalization. An increase in interference by the US Fed's monetary policy may also cause great uncertainties in terms of market expectations regarding the pace of the US Fed rate hikes. Moreover, geo–political conflicts and rising international terrorism may trigger tensions in related areas. On the other hand, factors contributing to balanced capital flows will play an active role. First, the domestic economic performance is improving and potential risks are under control. Active implementation of the opening–up policies is attracting more foreign investments. Improvements in the foreign–investment environment are in place. These factors will attract more long–term capital inflows. Second, with the strengthening of Chinese enterprises and the rising demand to allocate resources globally, China's outward foreign direct investments will grow at a high speed. After a short period of accelerated going–out, Chinese enterprises will be more cautious about investment risks and will be more rational and stable when investing abroad. Third, in order to open up more financial markets China has implemented macro–prudential cross–border financing management, has further opened up the inter–bank bond market, and has deepened foreign–exchange management of QFIIs and RQFIIs. These policies will gradually have an impact, and cross–border capital will continue to flow into China. Fourth, with progress in the market formation of the RMB exchange–rate regime, RMB exchange rates will become more flexible, contributing to two–way cross–border capital flows.

In 2017, foreign–exchange administration will abide by the overall goals of stability and progress and will balance between facilitating and guarding against risks. On the one hand, the authorities will continue to deepen foreign–exchange administration reforms, promote foreign–exchange market reforms, further open up financial markets, facilitate trade and investment, and better serve the real economy. On the other hand, the authorities will reinforce guidance of market participants' duty to strictly abide by the authenticity of their compliance with audits. They will also strictly fight against illegal foreign–exchange activities and reinforce interim and ex post management, improve the framework for macro–prudential management of cross–border flows, guard against risks underlying cross–border flows, and support the healthy and sound development of the foreign–exchange markets.

附 录 统计资料
Appendix Statistics

一、国际收支^①

I. Balance of Payments

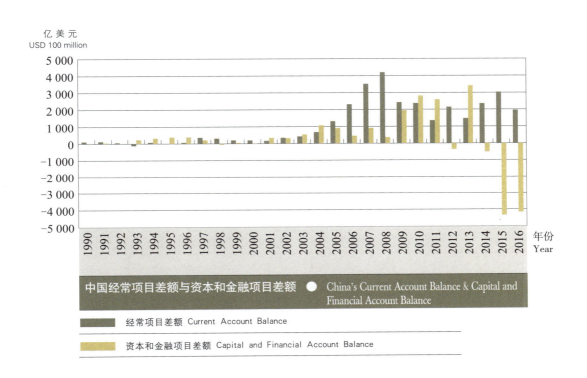

亿 美 元
USD 100 million

中国经常项目差额与资本和金融项目差额 ● China's Current Account Balance & Capital and Financial Account Balance

经常项目差额 Current Account Balance

资本和金融项目差额 Capital and Financial Account Balance

---

① 资料来源：国家外汇管理局；IMF《国际收支统计》、《国际金融统计》；环亚经济数据库。

Sources: State Administration of Foreign Exchange; IMF, *Balance of Payments Statistics*, *International Financial Statistics*; CEIC Database.

中国国际收支概览表（1）

China's Balance of Payments Abridged (1)

项目　年份 Item/Year	1982	1983	1984	1985	1986	1987
1.经常账户Current account	57	42	20	−114	−70	3
贷方Credit	243	240	273	276	276	354
借方Debit	−186	−198	−253	−390	−347	−351
A.货物和服务Goods and services	48	26	1	−125	−74	3
贷方Credit	226	220	248	258	262	341
借方Debit	−178	−194	−247	−383	−336	−338
a.货物Goods	42	18	−2	−131	−90	−13
贷方Credit	199	192	217	227	223	300
借方Debit	−158	−174	−219	−358	−313	−313
b.服务Services	6	8	2	6	16	16
贷方Credit	27	28	31	31	39	41
借方Debit	−20	−20	−29	−25	−23	−25
B.初次收入Primary income	4	12	15	8	0	−2
贷方Credit	10	15	19	14	9	10
借方Debit	−6	−3	−4	−5	−9	−12
C.二次收入Secondary income	5	5	4	2	4	2
贷方Credit	7	6	6	4	5	4
借方Debit	−2	−1	−2	−2	−1	−2
2.资本和金融账户 Capital and financial account	−60	−41	−32	139	83	11
2.1 资本账户Capital account	0	0	0	0	0	0
贷方Credit	0	0	0	0	0	0
借方Debit	0	0	0	0	0	0
2.2 金融账户Financial account	−60	−41	−32	139	83	11

单位：亿美元
Unit: USD 100 million

项目　年份 Item/Year	1982	1983	1984	1985	1986	1987
资产Credit	−71	−54	−58	50	13	−58
负债Debit	11	13	25	89	70	69
2.2.1 非储备性质的金融账户 Financial account excluding reserve assets	−17	−14	−38	85	65	27
资产Credit	−29	−27	−63	−4	−4	−42
负债Debit	11	13	25	89	70	69
直接投资Direct investment	4	8	13	13	18	17
资产Credit	0	−1	−1	−6	−5	−6
负债Debit	4	9	14	20	22	23
证券投资Portfolio investment	0	−6	−16	30	16	11
资产Credit	0	−6	−17	23	0	−1
负债Debit	0	0	1	8	16	12
金融衍生工具 Financial derivatives (other than reserves) and employee stock options	0	0	0	0	0	0
资产Credit	0	0	0	0	0	0
负债Debit	0	0	0	0	0	0
其他投资Other investment	−21	−16	−34	41	32	0
资产Assets	−28	−19	−44	−20	1	−34
负债Liabilities	6	4	10	62	31	34
2.2.2 储备资产Reserve assets	−42	−27	5	54	17	−17
其中：外汇储备 Foreign exchange reserves	−43	−19	7	56	12	−15
3.净误差与遗漏 Net errors and omissions	3	−2	12	−25	−12	−14

中国国际收支概览表（2）

China's Balance of Payments Abridged(2)

项目 / 年份 Item / Year	1994	1995	1996	1997	1998	1999
1.经常账户 **Current account**	77	16	72	370	315	211
贷方Credit	1 121	1 389	1 645	1 986	1 990	2 124
借方Debit	−1 045	−1 373	−1 573	−1 617	−1 675	−1 913
A.货物和服务 **Goods and services**	74	120	176	428	438	306
贷方Credit	1 046	1 319	1 548	1 874	1 888	1 987
借方Debit	−973	−1 199	−1 373	−1 446	−1 449	−1 681
a.货物Goods	35	128	122	366	456	329
贷方Credit	844	1 074	1 268	1 532	1 637	1 693
借方Debit	−810	−947	−1 147	−1 167	−1 181	−1 364
b.服务Services	39	−8	54	63	−18	−23
贷方Credit	202	244	280	342	251	294
借方Debit	−163	−252	−226	−280	−268	−317
B.初次收入 **Primary income**	−10	−118	−124	−110	−166	−145
贷方Credit	57	52	73	57	56	83
借方Debit	−68	−170	−198	−167	−222	−228
C.二次收入 **Secondary income**	13	14	21	51	43	49
贷方Credit	18	18	24	55	47	54
借方Debit	−4	−4	−2	−3	−4	−4
2.资本和金融账户 **Capital and financial account**	21	162	83	−147	−127	−33
2.1 资本账户 **Capital account**	0	0	0	0	0	0
贷方Credit	0	0	0	0	0	0
借方Debit	0	0	0	0	0	0
2.2 金融账户 **Financial account**	21	162	83	−147	−127	−33

单位：亿美元
Unit: USD 100 million

项目 / 年份 Item / Year	1994	1995	1996	1997	1998	1999
资产Credit	−367	−247	−357	−788	−479	−452
负债Debit	389	409	440	641	352	419
2.2.1 非储备性质的金融账户 Financial account excluding reserve assets	326	387	400	210	−63	52
资产Credit	−62	−22	−40	−431	−415	−367
负债Debit	389	409	440	641	352	419
直接投资 Direct investment	318	338	381	417	411	370
资产Credit	−20	−20	−21	−26	−26	−18
负债Debit	338	358	402	442	438	388
证券投资 Portfolio investment	35	8	17	69	−37	−112
资产Credit	−4	1	−6	−9	−38	−105
负债Debit	39	7	24	78	1	−7
金融衍生工具 Financial derivatives (other than reserves) and employee stock options	0	0	0	0	0	0
资产Credit	0	0	0	0	0	0
负债Debit	0	0	0	0	0	0
其他投资 Other investment	−27	40	2	−276	−437	−205
资产Assets	−38	−3	−13	−396	−350	−244
负债Liabilities	12	43	15	120	−86	39
2.2.2 储备资产 Reserve assets	−305	−225	−317	−357	−64	−85
其中:外汇储备 Foreign exchange reserves	−304	−220	−315	−349	−51	−97
3.净误差与遗漏 Net errors and omissions	−98	−178	−155	−223	−187	−178

中国国际收支概览表（3）

China's Balance of Payments Abridged (3)

项目/年份 Item / Year	2000	2001	2002	2003	2004	2005
1.经常账户 Current account	204	174	354	431	689	1 324
贷方Credit	2 725	2 906	3 551	4 825	6 522	8 403
借方Debit	−2 521	−2 732	−3 197	−4 395	−5 833	−7 080
A.货物和服务 Goods and services	288	281	374	358	512	1 246
贷方Credit	2 531	2 721	3 330	4 480	6 074	7 733
借方Debit	−2 243	−2 440	−2 956	−4 121	−5 562	−6 487
a.货物Goods	299	282	377	398	594	1 301
贷方Credit	2 181	2 329	2 868	3 966	5 429	6 949
借方Debit	−1 881	−2 047	−2 491	−3 568	−4 835	−5 647
b.服务Services	−11	−1	−3	−40	−82	−55
贷方Credit	350	392	462	513	645	785
借方Debit	−362	−393	−465	−553	−727	−840
B.初次收入 Primary income	−147	−192	−149	−102	−51	−161
贷方Credit	126	94	83	161	206	393
借方Debit	−272	−286	−233	−263	−257	−554
C.二次收入 Secondary income	63	85	130	174	229	239
贷方Credit	69	91	138	185	243	277
借方Debit	−5	−6	−8	−10	−14	−39
2.资本和金融账户 Capital and financial account	−86	−125	−432	−513	−819	−1 553
2.1 资本账户 Capital account	0	−1	0	0	−1	41
贷方Credit	0	0	0	0	0	42
借方Debit	0	−1	0	0	−1	−1

单位：亿美元
Unit: USD 100 million

项目 / 年份 Item / Year	2000	2001	2002	2003	2004	2005
2.2 金融账户 Financial account	−86	−125	−432	−512	−818	−1 594
资产Credit	−666	−541	−932	−1 212	−1 916	−3 352
负债Debit	580	416	500	699	1 098	1 758
2.2.1 非储备性质的 金融账户 Financial account excluding reserve assets	20	348	323	549	1 082	912
资产Credit	−561	−67	−177	−150	−16	−845
负债Debit	580	416	500	699	1 098	1 758
直接投资 Direct investment	375	374	468	494	601	904
资产Credit	−9	−69	−25	0	−20	−137
负债Debit	384	442	493	495	621	1 041
证券投资 Portfolio investment	−40	−194	−103	114	197	−47
资产Credit	−113	−207	−121	30	65	−262
负债Debit	73	12	18	84	132	214
金融衍生工具 Financial derivatives (other than reserves) and employee stock options	0	0	0	0	0	0
资产Credit	0	0	0	0	0	0
负债Debit	0	0	0	0	0	0
其他投资 Other investment	−315	169	−41	−60	283	56
资产Assets	−439	208	−31	−180	−61	−447
负债Liabilities	123	−39	−10	120	345	502
2.2.2 储备资产 Reserve assets	−105	−473	−755	−1 061	−1 901	−2 506
其中:外汇储备 Foreign exchange reserves	−109	−466	−742	−1 060	−1 904	−2 526
3.净误差与遗漏 Net errors and omissions	−119	−49	78	82	130	229

中国国际收支概览表（4）

China's Balance of Payments Abridged (4)

项目 / 年份 Item / Year	2006	2007	2008	2009	2010	2011
1.经常账户Current account	2 318	3 532	4 206	2 433	2 378	1 361
贷方Credit	10 779	13 832	16 597	14 006	17 959	22 087
借方Debit	−8 460	−10 300	−12 391	−11 574	−15 581	−20 726
A.货物和服务Goods and services	2 089	3 080	3 488	2 201	2 230	1 819
贷方Credit	9 917	12 571	14 953	12 497	16 039	20 089
借方Debit	−7 828	−9 490	−11 465	−10 296	−13 809	−18 269
a.货物Goods	2 157	3 117	3 599	2 435	2 464	2 287
贷方Credit	8 977	11 316	13 500	11 272	14 864	18 078
借方Debit	−6 820	−8 199	−9 901	−8 836	−12 400	−15 791
b.服务Services	−68	−37	−111	−234	−234	−468
贷方Credit	941	1 254	1 453	1 226	1 175	2 010
借方Debit	−1 008	−1 291	−1 564	−1 460	−1 409	−2 478
B.初次收入Primary income	−51	80	286	−85	−259	−703
贷方Credit	546	835	1 118	1 083	1 424	1 443
借方Debit	−597	−754	−832	−1 168	−1 683	−2 146
C.二次收入Secondary income	281	371	432	317	407	245
贷方Credit	316	426	526	426	495	556
借方Debit	−35	−55	−94	−110	−88	−311
2.资本和金融账户 Capital and financial account	−2 355	−3 665	−4 394	−2 019	−1 849	−1 223
2.1 资本账户Capital account	40	31	31	39	46	54
贷方Credit	41	33	33	42	48	56
借方Debit	−1	−2	−3	−3	−2	−2
2.2 金融账户Financial account	−2 395	−3 696	−4 425	−2 058	−1 895	−1 278

单位：亿美元
Unit: USD 100 million

项目／年份 Item / Year	2006	2007	2008	2009	2010	2011
资产Credit	−4 519	−6 371	−6 087	−4 283	−6 536	−6 136
负债Debit	2 124	2 676	1 662	2 225	4 641	4 858
2.2.1 非储备性质的金融账户 Financial account excluding reserve assets	453	911	371	1 945	2 822	2 600
资产Credit	−1 671	−1 764	−1 291	−280	−1 819	−2 258
负债Debit	2 124	2 676	1 662	2 225	4 641	4 858
直接投资Direct investment	1 001	1 391	1 148	872	1 857	2 317
资产Credit	−239	−172	−567	−439	−580	−484
负债Debit	1 241	1 562	1 715	1 311	2 437	2 801
证券投资Portfolio investment	−684	164	349	271	240	196
资产Credit	−1 113	−45	252	−25	−76	62
负债Debit	429	210	97	296	317	134
金融衍生工具 Financial derivatives (other than reserves) and employee stock options	0	0	0	0	0	0
资产Credit	0	0	0	0	0	0
负债Debit	0	0	0	0	0	0
其他投资Other investment	136	−644	−1 126	803	724	87
资产Assets	−319	−1 548	−976	184	−1 163	−1 836
负债Liabilities	455	904	−150	619	1 887	1 923
2.2.2 储备资产Reserve assets	−2 848	−4 607	−4 795	−4 003	−4 717	−3 878
其中:外汇储备 Foreign exchange reserves	−2 853	−4 609	−4 783	−3 821	−4 696	−3 848
3.净误差与遗漏 Net errors and omissions	36	133	188	−414	−529	−138

中国国际收支概览表（5）

China's Balance of Payments Abridged (5)

项目/年份 Item / Year	2012	2013	2014	2015	2016
1.经常账户 Current account	2 154	1 482	2 197	3 306	1 964
贷方Credit	23 933	25 927	27 299	26 930	24 546
借方Debit	−21 779	−24 445	−25 102	−23 624	−22 583
A.货物和服务 Goods and services	2 318	2 354	2 840	3 846	2 499
贷方Credit	21 751	23 556	24 758	24 293	21 979
借方Debit	−19 432	−21 202	−21 917	−20 447	−19 480
a.货物Goods	3 116	3 590	4 350	5 670	4 941
贷方Credit	19 735	21 486	22 438	21 428	19 895
借方Debit	−16 619	−17 896	−18 087	−15 758	−14 954
b.服务Services	−797	−1 236	−1 510	−1 824	−2 442
贷方Credit	2 016	2 070	2 320	2 865	2 084
借方Debit	−2 813	−3 306	−3 830	−4 689	−4 526
B.初次收入 Primary income	−199	−784	−341	−454	−440
贷方Credit	1 670	1 840	2 130	2 278	2 258
借方Debit	−1 869	−2 624	−2 471	−2 732	−2 698
C.二次收入 Secondary income	34	−87	−302	−87	−95
贷方Credit	512	532	411	359	309
借方Debit	−477	−619	−714	−446	−404
2.资本和金融账户 Capital and financial account	−1 283	−853	−795	−1 424	263
2.1 资本账户 Capital account	43	31	0	3	−3
贷方Credit	45	45	19	5	3
借方Debit	−3	−14	−20	−2	−7

单位：亿美元
Unit: USD 100 million

项目 / 年份 Item / Year	2012	2013	2014	2015	2016
2.2 金融账户 Financial account	−1 326	−883	−795	−1 427	267
资产Credit	−3 996	−6 517	−5 120	−491	−2 174
负债Debit	2 670	5 633	4 325	−936	2 441
2.2.1 非储备性质的金融账户 Financial account excluding reserve assets	−360	3 430	383	−4 856	−4 170
资产Credit	−3 030	−2 203	−3 942	−3 920	−6 611
负债Debit	2 670	5 633	4 325	−936	2 441
直接投资 Direct investment	1 763	2 180	2 087	621	−466
资产Credit	−650	−730	−804	−1 878	−2 172
负债Debit	2 412	2 909	2 891	2 499	1 706
证券投资 Portfolio investment	478	529	824	−665	−622
资产Credit	−64	−54	−108	−732	−1 034
负债Debit	542	582	932	67	412
金融衍生工具 Financial derivatives (other than reserves) and employee stock options	0	0	0	−21	−47
资产Credit	0	0	0	−34	−69
负债Debit	0	0	0	13	22
其他投资 Other investment	−2 601	722	−2 528	−4 791	−3 035
资产Assets	−2 317	−1 420	−3 030	−1 276	−3 336
负债Liabilities	−284	2 142	502	−3 515	301
2.2.2 储备资产 Reserve assets	−966	−4 314	−1 178	3 429	4 437
其中:外汇储备 Foreign exchange reserves	−987	−4 327	−1 188	3 423	4 487
3.净误差与遗漏 Net errors and omissions	−871	−629	669	2 130	−2 227

2016年中国国际收支平衡表

China's Balance of Payments in the 2016

项目 Item	行次 Line No.	2016年 Year
1. 经常账户Current account	1	1 964
贷方Credit	2	24 546
借方Debit	3	−22 583
1.A 货物和服务Goods and services	4	2 499
贷方Credit	5	21 979
借方Debit	6	−19 480
1.A.a 货物Goods	7	4 941
贷方Credit	8	19 895
借方Debit	9	−14 954
1.A.b 服务Services	10	−2 442
贷方Credit	11	2 084
借方Debit	12	−4 526
1.A.b.1 加工服务 Manufacturing services on physical inputs owned by others	13	184
贷方Credit	14	185
借方Debit	15	−2
1.A.b.2 维护和维修服务 Maintenance and repair services n.i.e	16	32
贷方Credit	17	52
借方Debit	18	−20
1.A.b.3 运输Transport	19	−468
贷方Credit	20	338
借方Debit	21	−806
1.A.b.4 旅行Travel	22	−2 167
贷方Credit	23	444
借方Debit	24	−2 611
1.A.b.5 建设Construction	25	42
贷方Credit	26	127
借方Debit	27	−85
1.A.b.6 保险和养老金服务 Insurance and pension services	28	−88
贷方Credit	29	41
借方Debit	30	−129
1.A.b.7 金融服务Financial services	31	11

单位：亿美元
Unit: USD 100 million

项目 Item	行次 Line No.	2016年 Year
贷方 Credit	32	32
借方 Debit	33	−20
1.A.b.8 知识产权使用费 Charges for the use of intellectual property	34	−228
贷方 Credit	35	12
借方 Debit	36	−240
1.A.b.9 电信、计算机和信息服务 Telecommunications, computer, and information services	37	127
贷方 Credit	38	254
借方 Debit	39	−127
1.A.b.10 其他商业服务 Other business services	40	147
贷方 Credit	41	580
借方 Debit	42	−432
1.A.b.11 个人、文化和娱乐服务 Personal, cultural, and recreational services	43	−14
贷方 Credit	44	7
借方 Debit	45	−21
1.A.b.12 别处未提及的政府服务 Government goods and services n.i.e	46	−20
贷方 Credit	47	12
借方 Debit	48	−32
1.B 初次收入 Primary income	49	−440
贷方 Credit	50	2 258
借方 Debit	51	−2 698
1.B.1 雇员报酬 Compensation of employees	52	207
贷方 Credit	53	269
借方 Debit	54	−62
1.B.2 投资收益 Investment income	55	−650
贷方 Credit	56	1 984
借方 Debit	57	−2 634
1.B.3 其他初次收入 Other primary income	58	3
贷方 Credit	59	6
借方 Debit	60	−2

2016年中国国际收支平衡表

China's Balance of Payments in the 2016

项目 Item	行次 Line No.	2016年 Year
1.C 二次收入Secondary income	61	−95
贷方Credit	62	309
借方Debit	63	−404
2. 资本和金融账户Capital and financial account	64	263
2.1 资本账户Capital account	65	−3
贷方Credit	66	3
借方Debit	67	−7
2.2 金融账户Financial account	68	267
资产Assets	69	−2 174
负债Liabilities	70	2 441
2.2.1 非储备性质的金融账户 Financial account excluding reserve assets	71	−4 170
资产Assets	72	−6 611
负债Liabilities	73	2 441
2.2.1.1 直接投资Direct investment	74	−466
2.2.1.1.1 直接投资资产Assets	75	−2 172
2.2.1.1.1.1 股权 Equity and investment fund shares	76	−1 484
2.2.1.1.1.2 关联企业债务 Debt instruments	77	−688
2.2.1.1.2直接投资负债Liabilities	78	1 706
2.2.1.1.2.1 股权 Equity and investment fund shares	79	1 642
2.2.1.1.2.2 关联企业债务 Debt instruments	80	64
2.2.1.2 证券投资Portfolio investment	81	−622
2.2.1.2.1 资产Assets	82	−1 034
2.2.1.2.1.1 股权 Equity and investment fund shares	83	−385
2.2.1.2.1.2 债券Debt securities	84	−649
2.2.1.2.2 负债Liabilities	85	412
2.2.1.2.2.1 股权 Equity and investment fund shares	86	189
2.2.1.2.2.2 债券Debt securities	87	223
2.2.1.3 金融衍生工具Financial derivatives (other than reserves) and employee stock options	88	−47
2.2.1.3.1 资产Assets	89	−69
2.2.1.3.2 负债Liabilities	90	22
2.2.1.4 其他投资Other investment	91	−3 035
2.2.1.4.1 资产Assets	92	−3 336

单位：亿美元
Unit: USD 100 million

项目 Item	行次 Line No.	2016年 Year
2.2.1.4.1.1 其他股权Other equity	93	0
2.2.1.4.1.2 货币和存款 Currency and deposits	94	−435
2.2.1.4.1.3 贷款Loans	95	−1 147
2.2.1.4.1.4 保险和养老金 Insurance, pension, and standardized guarantee schemes	96	−3
2.2.1.4.1.5 贸易信贷 Trade credit and advances	97	−1 008
2.2.1.4.1.6 其他应收款 Other accounts receivable	98	−743
2.2.1.4.2 负债Liabilities	99	301
2.2.1.4.2.1 其他股权Other equity	100	0
2.2.1.4.2.2 货币和存款 Currency and deposits	101	102
2.2.1.4.2.3 贷款Loans	102	−196
2.2.1.4.2.4 保险和养老金 Insurance, pension, and standardized guarantee schemes	103	−6
2.2.1.4.2.5 贸易信贷 Trade credit and advances	104	162
2.2.1.4.2.6 其他应付款 Other accounts payable	105	239
2.2.1.4.2.7 特别提款权 Special drawing rights	106	0
2.2.2 储备资产Reserve assets	107	4 437
2.2.2.1 货币黄金Monetary gold	108	0
2.2.2.2 特别提款权Special drawing rights	109	3
2.2.2.3 在国际货币基金组织的储备头寸 Reserve position in the IMF	110	−53
2.2.2.4 外汇储备Foreign exchange reserves	111	4 487
2.2.2.5其他储备资产Other reserve assets	112	0
3.净误差与遗漏Net errors and omissions	113	−2 227

美国国际收支概览表

Balance of Payments Abridged of United States

项目 Item / 年份 Year	2008	2009	2010	2011	2012	2013	2014	2015	2016
一、经常项目差额 Current Account Balance	−690.79	−384.02	−441.96	−460.36	−446.53	−366.42	−392.07	−462.96	−481.21
贷方 Credit	2 751.95	2 285.92	2 630.80	2 987.57	3 097.06	3 214.80	3 338.76	3 172.69	3 142.17
借方 Debit	3 442.74	2 669.94	3 072.76	3 447.93	3 543.59	3 581.22	3 730.82	3 635.65	3 623.38
A.货物和服务差额 Goods and Services Balance	−708.73	−383.78	−494.66	−548.63	−536.77	−461.88	−490.18	−500.35	−500.56
贷方 Credit	1 841.61	1 583.05	1 853.60	2 127.02	2 218.99	2 293.45	2 376.58	2 261.17	2 212.08
借方 Debit	2 550.34	1 966.83	2 348.26	2 675.65	2 755.76	2 755.33	2 866.76	2 761.52	2 712.64
a.货物差额 Goods Balance	−832.49	−509.70	−648.68	−740.64	−741.17	−702.24	−752.17	−762.57	−749.93
贷方 Credit	1 308.79	1 070.33	1 290.27	1 499.24	1 562.58	1 592.00	1 633.32	1 510.30	1 459.67
借方 Debit	2 141.29	1 580.03	1 938.95	2 239.88	2 303.75	2 294.25	2 385.49	2 272.87	2 209.59
b.服务差额 Services Balance	123.76	125.92	154.02	192.02	204.40	240.37	261.99	262.21	249.37
贷方 Credit	532.82	512.72	563.33	627.78	656.41	701.45	743.26	750.86	752.41
借方 Debit	409.06	386.80	409.31	435.76	452.01	461.08	481.27	488.65	503.05
B.初次收入差额 Primary Income Balance	146.15	123.59	177.66	220.96	215.79	218.97	224.00	182.38	180.59
贷方 Credit	823.71	614.38	684.91	759.73	768.96	794.66	821.81	782.92	801.92
借方 Debit	677.56	490.79	507.25	538.77	553.17	575.69	597.80	600.53	621.34
C.二次收入差额 Secondary Income Balance	−128.21	−123.83	−124.96	−132.69	−125.55	−123.52	−125.89	−144.99	−161.24
贷方 Credit	86.63	88.49	92.28	100.82	109.12	126.69	140.37	128.61	128.17
借方 Debit	214.84	212.32	217.24	233.51	234.66	250.20	266.26	273.60	289.41
二、资本项目差额 Capital Account Balance	6.01	−0.14	−0.16	−1.19	6.90	−0.41	−0.05	−0.04	−0.06
三、金融项目净贷出（+）/净借入（−） Financial Account Net Lending(+)/Net Borrow(−)	−730.58	−230.94	−436.98	−515.65	−440.53	−390.97	−287.38	−195.24	−406.45
1.直接投资差额 Direct Investment Balance	18.99	159.94	95.23	183.00	135.21	117.66	136.07	−30.79	−77.73

单位：10亿美元
Unit: USD billion

项目　　　　年份 Item　　　　Year	2008	2009	2010	2011	2012	2013	2014	2015	2016
1.1资产 Assets	351.72	313.73	354.58	440.41	378.22	394.64	343.44	348.65	347.53
1.2负债 Liabilities	332.73	153.79	259.34	257.41	243.01	276.98	207.37	379.43	425.26
2.证券投资差额 Portfolio Investment Balance	−807.95	18.53	−620.82	−226.26	−498.25	−30.69	−119.17	−96.97	−250.24
2.1资产 Assets	−284.27	375.88	199.62	85.36	248.76	481.30	582.69	153.97	20.68
2.2负债 Liabilities	523.68	357.35	820.43	311.63	747.01	511.98	701.86	250.94	270.92
3.金融衍生产品 （储备除外） 和雇员认股权差额 Derivatives (other than reserves) and Employee Stock Options Balance	32.95	−44.82	−14.08	−35.01	7.06	2.22	−54.35	−25.39	21.95
4.其他投资差额 Other Investment Balance	20.60	−416.78	100.85	−453.36	−89.02	−477.08	−246.35	−35.79	−102.53
4.1资产 Assets	−381.77	−609.66	407.42	−45.33	−453.70	−221.41	−99.20	−270.92	−39.34
4.2负债 Liabilities	−402.37	−192.88	306.57	408.04	−364.68	255.67	147.14	−235.14	63.19
5.储备资产差额 Reserve Assets Balance	4.84	52.18	⊦.83	15.98	4.46	−3.09	−3.58	−6.30	2.10
四、净误差与遗漏 Net Errors and Omissions	−45.81	153.22	5.14	−54.11	−0.91	−24.14	104.73	267.77	74.82

德国国际收支概览表

Balance of Payments Abridged of Germany

项目 Item / 年份 Year	2008	2009	2010	2011	2012	2013	2014	2015	2016
一、经常项目差额 Current Account Balance	210.89	198.87	193.03	227.97	248.92	253.48	281.30	279.97	289.16
贷方 Credit	1 996.32	1 609.18	1 765.77	2 062.61	1 960.65	2 041.26	2 106.94	1 857.18	1 884.44
借方 Debit	1 785.42	1 410.31	1 572.74	1 834.63	1 711.72	1 787.78	1 825.64	1 577.21	1 595.28
A.货物和服务差额 Goods and Services Balance	226.62	170.60	178.33	181.70	215.61	223.80	253.44	253.26	276.10
贷方 Credit	1 639.84	1 297.26	1 444.67	1 683.35	1 629.56	1 706.02	1 771.50	1 570.13	1 603.56
借方 Debit	1 413.22	1 126.65	1 266.35	1 501.65	1 413.95	1 482.21	1 518.06	1 316.88	1 327.47
a.货物差额 Goods Balance	273.83	198.01	213.74	227.28	257.42	281.06	300.41	287.89	301.01
贷方 Credit	1 398.44	1 074.45	1 217.09	1 432.93	1 377.08	1 434.13	1 480.22	1 305.67	1 322.35
借方 Debit	1 124.61	876.44	1 003.34	1 205.65	1 119.65	1 153.07	1 179.82	1 017.79	1 021.34
b.服务差额 Services Balance	−47.21	−27.41	−35.41	−45.58	−41.81	−57.26	−46.97	−34.63	−24.91
贷方 Credit	241.40	222.81	227.59	250.42	252.48	271.89	291.27	264.46	281.21
借方 Debit	288.61	250.21	263.00	296.00	294.30	329.14	338.24	299.09	306.12
B.初次收入差额 Primary Income Balance	34.19	77.26	68.08	95.30	84.74	87.84	81.85	70.68	57.16
贷方 Credit	290.61	255.48	264.98	306.42	263.22	255.86	253.83	216.01	208.86
借方 Debit	256.43	178.22	196.90	211.12	178.48	168.02	171.98	145.33	151.69
C.二次收入差额 Secondary Income Balance	−49.91	−48.99	−53.37	−49.03	−51.43	−58.16	−53.99	−43.97	−44.10
贷方 Credit	65.87	56.45	56.11	72.84	67.87	79.39	81.62	71.04	72.03
借方 Debit	115.78	105.44	109.49	121.87	119.30	137.55	135.61	115.01	116.13
二、资本项目差额 Capital Account Balance	−1.22	−2.60	1.62	2.25	−0.61	−0.86	1.77	−0.14	1.26
三、金融项目净贷出（＋）/净借入（−） Financial Account Net Lending(+)/Net Borrow(−)	179.85	184.43	123.74	167.70	185.79	291.57	323.94	249.68	253.53
1.直接投资差额 Direct Investment Balance	67.06	42.99	60.64	10.35	33.65	28.06	105.59	62.61	23.79
1.1资产 Assets	97.99	99.65	146.69	107.83	99.11	90.77	115.03	108.84	76.26
1.2负债 Liabilities	30.93	56.67	86.05	97.48	65.46	62.71	9.44	46.23	52.47

单位：10亿美元
Unit: USD billion

项目　年份 Item　Year	2008	2009	2010	2011	2012	2013	2014	2015	2016
2.证券投资差额 Portfolio Investment Balance	−44.54	119.24	154.11	−51.41	66.85	212.80	180.57	220.34	230.45
2.1资产 Assets	−14.74	110.19	230.22	25.56	136.16	186.02	198.39	138.26	107.65
2.2负债 Liabilities	29.80	−9.05	76.11	76.97	69.32	−26.78	17.82	−82.08	−122.80
3.金融衍生产品（储备除外）和雇员认股权差额 Derivatives (other than reserves) and Employee Stock Options Balance	43.99	−7.54	17.57	39.76	30.92	31.88	42.09	28.71	36.08
3.1资产 Assets	43.99	−7.54	17.57	39.76	30.92	31.88	42.09	28.71	36.08
3.2负债 Liabilities	0.00	0.00	0.00	0.00	0.00	0.00	0.00	0.00	0.00
4.其他投资差额 Other Investment Balance	110.60	17.39	−110.71	165.09	52.68	17.68	−1.02	−59.55	−36.79
4.1资产 Assets	219.96	−145.51	156.88	194.47	217.56	−231.47	53.79	13.03	204.16
4.2负债 Liabilities	109.36	−162.91	267.59	29.38	164.89	−249.15	54.80	72.58	240.96
5.储备资产差额 Reserve Assets Balance	2.74	12.36	2.13	3.92	1.70	1.16	−3.30	−2.42	1.90
四、净误差与遗漏 Net Errors and Omissions	−29.83	−11.84	−70.91	−62.52	−62.52	38.95	40.86	−30.14	−32.47

英国国际收支概览表

Balance of Payments Abridged of United kingdom

项目 Item / 年份 Year	2008	2009	2010	2011	2012	2013	2014	2015	2016
一、经常项目差额 Current Account Balance	−101.33	−68.74	−66.84	−46.32	−97.08	−119.92	−139.69	−122.57	−1 15.53
贷方 Credit	1 363.77	929.79	986.48	1 146.90	1 089.33	1 091.37	1 108.31	1 025.23	960.19
借方 Debit	1 465.11	998.52	1 053.32	1 193.22	1 186.41	1 211.29	1 248.00	1 147.81	1 075.71
A.货物和服务差额 Goods and Services Balance	−87.54	−53.50	−65.94	−43.27	−59.00	−61.65	−59.62	−45.69	−50.20
贷方 Credit	779.98	623.67	687.04	796.50	788.47	809.41	842.15	790.50	739.79
借方 Debit	867.52	677.17	752.97	839.77	847.47	871.07	901.77	836.19	790.00
a.货物差额 Goods Balance	−176.85	−135.12	−150.76	−152.17	−175.23	−188.97	−201.57	−182.88	−181.17
贷方 Credit	472.85	358.65	417.81	493.74	476.43	474.06	482.01	439.35	407.22
借方 Debit	649.70	493.78	568.57	645.91	651.66	663.03	683.57	622.23	588.39
b.服务差额 Services Balance	89.31	81.62	84.83	108.90	116.23	127.32	141.95	137.19	130.96
贷方 Credit	307.13	265.02	269.23	302.76	312.04	335.36	360.14	351.15	332.57
借方 Debit	217.82	183.39	184.40	193.86	195.81	208.04	218.19	213.96	201.61
B.初次收入差额 Primary Income Balance	12.80	9.32	31.16	31.59	−3.48	−16.21	−39.07	−39.22	−32.36
贷方 Credit	546.35	279.97	275.39	327.62	274.87	251.28	234.46	204.37	192.89
借方 Debit	533.55	270.64	244.22	296.03	278.36	267.49	273.52	243.59	225.25
C.二次收入差额 Secondary Income Balance	−26.60	−24.56	−32.07	−34.65	−34.60	−42.06	−41.00	−37.66	−32.97
贷方 Credit	37.45	26.15	24.06	22.78	25.99	30.67	31.71	30.37	27.50
借方 Debit	64.04	50.71	56.13	57.43	60.59	72.73	72.71	68.03	60.47
二、资本项目差额 Capital Account Balance	0.46	0.64	0.00	−0.59	−0.27	−0.78	−0.66	−1.69	−2.43
三、金融项目净贷出（+）/净借入（−） Financial Account Net Lending(+)/Net Borrow(−)	−69.77	−44.94	−47.24	−34.49	−83.91	−123.85	−129.80	−103.12	−143.00
1.直接投资差额 Direct Investment Balance	103.24	−62.95	−12.33	53.82	−34.73	−8.22	−190.74	−114.50	−258.38
1.1资产 Assets	356.70	−48.40	54.41	80.83	12.02	46.25	−119.38	−56.05	41.29
1.2负债 Liabilities	253.45	14.55	66.73	27.01	46.75	54.47	71.36	58.45	299.67
2.证券投资差额 Portfolio Investment Balance	−433.42	−43.32	23.45	11.82	336.70	−87.50	−204.82	−415.14	−263.58
2.1资产 Assets	−180.44	280.54	159.91	20.56	207.84	−14.57	11.50	−46.34	−220.44
2.2负债 Liabilities	252.98	323.86	136.46	8.74	−128.87	72.93	216.32	368.81	43.14

单位：10亿美元
Unit: USD billion

项目 Item　年份 Year	2008	2009	2010	2011	2012	2013	2014	2015	2016
3.金融衍生产品（储备除外）和雇员认股权差额 Derivatives (other than reserves) and Employee Stock Options Balance	219.23	−49.08	−38.51	4.26	−58.10	17.98	−1.62	−47.98	34.27
4.其他投资差额 Other Investment Balance	44.26	100.85	−29.86	−115.27	−339.41	−53.06	257.24	443.19	336.04
4.1资产 Assets	−1 079.99	−529.83	362.12	167.79	−370.44	−327.31	185.76	−147.23	173.25
4.2负债 Liabilities	−1 124.25	−630.67	391.99	283.06	−31.02	−274.25	−71.48	−590.42	−162.79
5.储备资产差额 Reserve Assets Balance	−3.07	9.56	10.01	10.87	11.63	6.96	10.14	31.32	8.65
四、净误差与遗漏 Net Errors and Omissions	31.10	23.15	19.60	12.42	13.44	−3.15	10.54	21.15	−25.05

巴西国际收支概览表

Balance of Payments Abridged of Brazil

项目 Item / 年份 Year	2008	2009	2010	2011	2012	2013	2014	2015	2016
一、经常项目差额 Current Account Balance	−28.19	−24.31	−75.76	−76.97	−74.06	−74.79	−104.18	−58.88	−23.53
贷方 Credit	246.22	194.30	254.52	320.34	294.49	297.56	281.84	240.51	234.58
借方 Debit	274.41	218.61	330.28	397.31	368.55	372.35	386.02	299.39	258.11
A.货物和服务差额 Goods and Services Balance	8.15	6.03	−11.60	−9.48	−22.59	−45.93	−54.74	−19.25	14.59
贷方 Credit	228.39	180.72	232.06	292.55	281.26	279.64	264.06	223.87	217.75
借方 Debit	220.25	174.70	243.66	302.03	303.85	325.57	318.80	243.12	203.16
a.货物差额 Goods Balance	24.84	25.27	18.43	27.56	17.26	0.34	−6.63	17.67	45.04
贷方 Credit	197.94	152.99	201.26	255.44	242.12	241.53	224.10	190.09	184.45
借方 Debit	173.11	127.72	182.83	227.88	224.86	241.19	230.73	172.42	139.42
b.服务差额 Services Balance	−16.69	−19.25	−30.03	−37.04	−39.85	−46.27	−48.11	−36.92	−30.45
贷方 Credit	30.45	27.73	30.80	37.11	39.14	38.11	39.97	33.78	33.30
借方 Debit	47.14	46.97	60.83	74.15	78.98	84.38	88.07	70.70	63.75
B.初次收入差额 Primary Income Balance	−40.56	−33.67	−67.05	−70.48	−54.31	−32.54	−52.17	−42.36	−41.08
贷方 Credit	12.51	8.84	17.70	22.88	8.62	12.13	12.85	11.93	11.53
借方 Debit	53.07	42.51	84.75	93.36	62.93	44.67	65.02	54.29	52.61
C.二次收入差额 Secondary Income Balance	4.22	3.34	2.90	2.98	2.84	3.68	2.72	2.72	2.96
贷方 Credit	5.32	4.74	4.77	4.91	4.62	5.79	4.93	4.71	5.30
借方 Debit	1.09	1.40	1.87	1.92	1.78	2.11	2.21	1.99	2.34
二、资本项目差额 Capital Account Balance	−0.01	0.06	0.24	0.26	0.21	0.32	0.23	0.44	0.27
三、金融项目净贷出（+）/净借入（−） Financial Account Net Lending(+)/Net Borrow(−)	−25.33	−22.59	−75.92	−78.98	−73.93	−72.42	−100.60	−54.73	−16.47
1.直接投资差额 Direct Investment Balance	−24.60	−36.03	−61.69	−85.09	−81.40	−54.24	−70.86	−61.58	−71.11
1.1资产 Assets	26.12	−4.55	26.76	16.07	5.21	14.94	26.04	13.50	7.82

单位：10亿美元
Unit: USD billion

项目 Item \ 年份 Year	2008	2009	2010	2011	2012	2013	2014	2015	2016
1.2负债 Liabilities	50.72	31.48	88.45	101.16	86.61	69.18	96.89	75.07	78.93
2.证券投资差额 Portfolio Investment Balance	−1.13	−50.28	−66.91	−41.25	−15.83	−32.79	−38.71	−22.05	19.22
2.1资产 Assets	−1.90	−4.12	4.74	−16.86	7.40	8.98	2.82	−3.55	−0.60
2.2负债 Liabilities	−0.77	46.16	71.65	24.39	23.23	41.77	41.53	18.50	−19.81
3.金融衍生产品（储备除外）和雇员认股权差额 Derivatives (other than reserves) and Employee Stock Options Balance	0.31	−0.16	0.11	0.00	−0.02	−0.11	1.57	3.45	−0.97
3.1资产 Assets	−0.30	−0.32	−0.36	−0.39	−0.30	−0.50	−7.61	−20.66	−13.87
3.2负债 Liabilities	−0.61	−0.17	−0.47	−0.38	−0.28	−0.39	−9.18	−24.11	−12.90
4.其他投资差额 Other Investment Balance	−2.87	16.31	3.49	−11.27	4.42	20.64	−3.44	23.87	27.16
4.1资产 Assets	5.27	30.30	40.45	36.05	23.87	39.69	50.67	44.00	33.44
4.2负债 Liabilities	8.14	13.99	36.96	47.33	19.44	19.05	54.10	20.13	0.00
5.储备资产差额 Reserve Assets Balance	2.97	47.58	49.08	58.63	18.90	−5.92	10.83	1.57	9.24
四、净误差与遗漏 Net Errors and Omissions	2.88	1.66	−0.40	−2.26	−0.08	2.05	3.35	3.71	6.79

俄罗斯国际收支概览表

Balance of Payments Abridged of Russia

项目 Item 年份 Year	2008	2009	2010	2011	2012	2013	2014	2015	2016
一、经常项目差额 Current Account Balance	103.94	50.38	67.45	97.27	71.28	33.43	57.51	68.94	25.01
贷方 Credit	592.60	382.72	487.16	629.90	653.99	651.47	627.37	440.45	381.32
借方 Debit	488.66	332.34	419.70	532.63	582.71	618.04	569.85	371.51	356.31
A.货物和服务差额 Goods and Services Balance	157.21	95.63	120.87	163.40	145.08	122.31	133.65	111.59	66.14
贷方 Credit	523.43	342.95	441.83	573.45	589.77	591.96	562.55	393.16	332.19
借方 Debit	366.23	247.32	320.96	410.05	444.70	469.65	428.90	281.57	266.05
a.货物差额 Goods Balance	177.63	113.23	146.99	196.85	191.66	180.57	188.93	148.51	90.01
贷方 Credit	466.30	297.15	392.67	515.41	527.43	521.84	496.81	341.47	281.68
借方 Debit	288.67	183.92	245.68	318.55	335.77	341.27	307.88	192.95	191.67
b.服务差额 Services Balance	−20.42	−17.60	−26.12	−33.46	−46.59	−58.26	−55.28	−36.92	−23.88
贷方 Credit	57.14	45.80	49.16	58.04	62.34	70.12	65.74	51.70	50.50
借方 Debit	77.56	63.40	75.28	91.50	108.93	128.38	121.02	88.62	74.38
B.初次收入差额 Primary Income Balance	−46.48	−39.74	−47.10	−60.40	−67.66	−79.60	−67.96	−36.93	−34.69
贷方 Credit	61.82	33.40	38.06	42.69	47.76	42.18	47.17	37.27	40.78
借方 Debit	108.30	73.14	85.17	103.09	115.42	121.78	115.13	74.20	75.47
C.二次收入差额 Secondary Income Balance	−6.79	−5.51	−6.32	−5.72	−6.13	−9.27	−8.18	−5.72	−6.44
贷方 Credit	7.35	6.37	7.26	13.77	16.46	17.33	17.64	10.02	8.35
借方 Debit	14.13	11.88	13.58	19.49	22.59	26.61	25.82	15.74	14.79
二、资本项目差额 Capital Account Balance	−0.10	−12.47	−0.04	0.13	−5.22	−0.39	−42.01	−0.31	−0.77
三、金融项目净贷出（＋）/ 净借入（－）Financial Account Net Lending(+)/Net Borrow(−)	100.70	31.52	58.28	88.76	55.69	24.13	23.50	71.69	21.36
1.直接投资差额 Direct Investment Balance	−19.12	6.70	9.45	11.77	−1.77	17.29	35.05	15.23	−10.40

单位：10亿美元
Unit: USD billion

项目 Item　年份 Year	2008	2009	2010	2011	2012	2013	2014	2015	2016
1.1资产 Assets	55.66	43.28	52.62	66.85	48.82	86.51	57.08	22.09	22.58
1.2负债 Liabilities	74.78	36.58	43.17	55.08	50.59	69.22	22.03	6.85	32.98
2.证券投资差额 Portfolio Investment Balance	35.69	1.88	1.50	15.28	−17.03	11.01	39.94	26.42	−2.37
2.1资产 Assets	7.77	10.60	3.44	9.84	2.28	11.76	16.74	13.55	0.65
2.2负债 Liabilities	−27.92	8.72	1.95	−5.44	19.31	0.75	−23.20	−12.87	3.02
3.金融衍生产品（储备除外）和雇员认股权差额 Derivatives (other than reserves) and Employee Stock Options Balance	1.37	3.24	1.84	1.39	1.36	0.35	5.31	7.43	0.45
3.1资产 Assets	−9.12	−9.89	−8.84	−16.44	−16.70	−8.49	−16.57	−21.22	−13.17
3.2负债 Liabilities	−10.49	−13.13	−10.68	−17.83	−18.05	−8.83	−21.88	−28.65	−13.62
4.其他投资差额 Other Investment Balance	121.68	16.33	8.74	47.68	43.11	17.57	50.74	20.90	25.43
4.1资产 Assets	185.78	−9.25	19.24	83.37	83.70	80.82	24.01	−15.52	−1.27
4.2负债 Liabilities	64.10	−25.58	10.49	35.69	40.59	63.26	−26.73	−36.42	−26.70
5.储备资产差额 Reserve Assets Balance	−38.92	3.36	36.75	12.64	30.02	−22.08	−107.55	1.70	8.24
四、净误差与遗漏 Net Errors and Omissions	−3.13	−6.40	−9.13	−8.65	−10.37	−8.90	7.99	3.05	−2.88

中国国际投资头寸表

China's International Investment Position

项目 Item	2008年末	2009年末	2010年末	2011年末	2012年末	2013年末	2014年末	2015年末	2016年末
净头寸Net	14 938	14 905	16 880	16 884	18 665	19 960	16 028	16 728	18 005
A.资产Assets	29 567	34 369	41 189	47 345	52 132	59 861	64 383	61 558	64 666
1.直接投资 Direct investment	1 857	2 458	3 172	4 248	5 319	6 605	8 826	10 959	13 172
1.1 股权Equity and investment fund shares	–	–	–	–	–	–	7 408	9 123	10 650
1.2 关联企业债务 Debt instruments	–	–	–	–	–	–	1 418	1 836	2 522
2.证券投资 Portfolio investment	2 525	2 428	2 571	2 044	2 406	2 585	2 625	2 613	3 651
2.1 股权 Equity and investment fund shares	214	546	630	864	1 298	1 530	1 613	1 620	2 149
2.2 债券Debt securities	2 311	1 882	1 941	1 180	1 108	1 055	1 012	993	1 502
3.金融衍生工具 Financial derivatives (other than reserves) and employee stock options	–	–	–	–	–	–	0	36	52
4.其他投资 Other investment	5 523	4 952	6 304	8 495	10 527	11 867	13 938	13 889	16 811
4.1 其他股权Other equity	–	–	–	–	–	–	0	1	1
4.2 货币和存款 Currency and deposits	1 529	1 310	2 051	2 942	3 906	3 751	4 453	3 598	3 816
4.3 贷款Loans	1 071	974	1 174	2 232	2 778	3 089	3 747	4 569	5 622
4.4 保险和养老金Insurance, pension, and standardized guarantee schemes	–	–	–	–	–	–	0	172	123
4.5 贸易信贷 Trade credit and advances	1 102	1 444	2 060	2 769	3 387	3 990	4 677	5 137	6 145
4.6 其他应收款 Other accounts receivable	1 821	1 224	1 018	552	457	1 038	1 061	412	1 105
5.储备资产Reserve assets	19 662	24 532	29 142	32 558	33 879	38 804	38 993	34 061	30 978
5.1 货币黄金Monetary gold	169	371	481	530	567	408	401	602	679
5.2 特别提款权 Special drawing rights	12	125	123	119	114	112	105	103	97
5.3 在国际货币基金组织的储备头寸 Reserve position in the IMF	20	44	64	98	82	71	57	45	96
5.4 外汇储备 Foreign currency reserves	19 460	23 992	28 473	31 811	33 116	38 213	38 430	33 304	30 105

单位：亿美元
Unit: USD 100 million

项目 Item	2008年末	2009年末	2010年末	2011年末	2012年末	2013年末	2014年末	2015年末	2016年末
5.5 其他储备资产 Other reserve assets	–	–	–	–	–	–	0	7	2
B.负债 Liabilities	14 629	19 464	24 308	30 461	33 467	39 901	48 355	44 830	46 660
1.直接投资 Direct investment	9 155	13 148	15 696	19 069	20 680	23 312	25 991	26 963	28 659
1.1 股权 Equity and investment fund shares	–	–	–	–	–	–	24 076	24 962	26 543
1.2 关联企业债务 Debt instruments	–	–	–	–	–	–	1 915	2 002	2 117
2.证券投资 Portfolio investment	1 677	1 900	2 239	2 485	3 361	3 865	7 962	8 170	8 086
2.1 股权 Equity and investment fund shares	1 505	1 748	2 061	2 114	2 619	2 977	6 513	5 971	5 927
2.2 债券 Debt securities	172	152	178	371	742	889	1 449	2 200	2 159
3.金融衍生工具 Financial derivatives (other than reserves) and employee stock options	–	–	–	–	–	–	0	53	66
4.其他投资 Other investment	3 796	4 416	6 373	8 907	9 426	12 724	14 402	9 643	9 849
4.1 其他股权 Other equity	–	–	–	–	–	–	0	0	0
4.2 货币和存款 Currency and deposits	918	937	1 650	2 477	2 446	3 466	5 030	3 267	3 156
4.3 贷款 Loans	1 030	1 636	2 389	3 724	3 680	5 642	5 720	3 293	3 236
4.4 保险和养老金 Insurance, pension, and standardized guarantee schemes	–	–	–	–	–	–	0	93	88
4.5 贸易信贷 Trade credit and advances	1 296	1 617	2 112	2 492	2 915	3 365	3 344	2 721	2 883
4.6 其他应付款 Other accounts payable	552	121	106	106	277	144	207	172	391
4.7 特别提款权 Special drawing rights	–	106	116	107	107	108	101	97	94

外汇储备

Foreign Exchange Reserves

单位：亿美元
Unit: USD 100 million

年份 year	外汇储备余额 Foreign Exchange Reserves	外汇储备增加额 Increase of Foreign Exchange Reserves
1990	111	55
1991	217	106
1992	194	−23
1993	212	18
1994	516	304
1995	736	220
1996	1 050	315
1997	1 399	348
1998	1 450	51
1999	1 547	97
2000	1 656	109
2001	2 122	466
2002	2 854	742
2003	4 033	1 168
2004	6 099	2 067
2005	8 189	2 090
2006	10 663	2 475
2007	15 282	4 619
2008	19 460	4 178
2009	23 992	4 531
2010	28 473	4 481
2011	31 811	3 338
2012	33 116	1 304
2013	38 213	5 097
2014	38 430	217
2015	33 304	−5 127
2016	30 105	−3 198

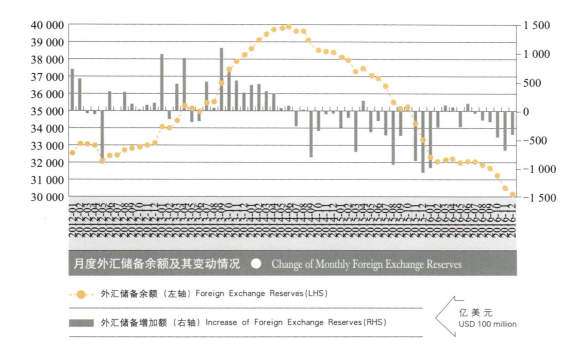

月度外汇储备余额及其变动情况 ● Change of Monthly Foreign Exchange Reserves

‑●‑ 外汇储备余额（左轴）Foreign Exchange Reserves（LHS）

■ 外汇储备增加额（右轴）Increase of Foreign Exchange Reserves（RHS）

亿 美 元
USD 100 million

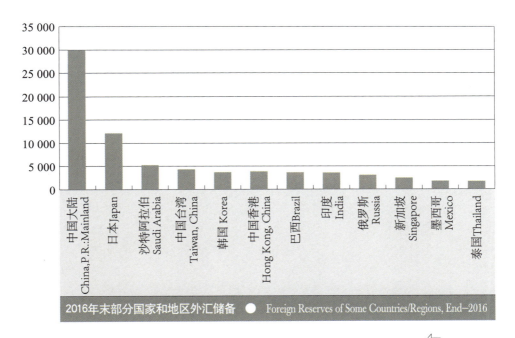

2016年末部分国家和地区外汇储备 ● Foreign Reserves of Some Countries/Regions, End‑2016

亿 美 元
USD 100 million

二、对外贸易①

II. Foreign Trade

2016年世界货物贸易出口前十名

Top 10 Countries/Regions of Goods Export in 2016

国家/地区 Countries/Regions	出口额（10亿美元） Export（USD billion）	增长 Increase（%）	占世界出口总额比重 Ratio to total Export of the world（%）	2015年排名 Ranking in 2015
世界World	15 955	−3	100	
1.中国P.R.C	2 098	−8	13.2	1
2.美国U.S.	1 455	−3	9.1	2
3.德国Germany	1 340	1	8.4	3
4.日本Japan	645	3	4	4
5.荷兰Netherlands	570	0	3.6	5
6.中国香港HongKong,SAR	517	1	3.2	7
7.法国France	501	−1	3.1	8
8.韩国Korea	495	−6	3.1	6
9.意大利Italy	465	1	2.9	10
10.英国UK	409	−1.1	2.6	9

① 数据来源：海关总署；世界贸易组织。
Sources: General Administration of Customs; World Trade Organization.

2016年世界货物贸易进口前十名

Top 10 Countries/Regions of Goods Import in 2016

国家/地区 Countries/Regions	进口额（10亿美元） Import（USD billion）	增长 Increase（%）	占世界进口总额比重 Ratio to total Import of the world（%）	2015年排名 Ranking in 2015
世界World	16 225	−3	100	
1.美国U.S.	2 551	−3	13.9	1
2.中国P.R.C	1 587	−5	9.8	2
3.德国Germany	1 055	−0	6.5	3
4.英国UK	636	1	3.9	5
5.日本Japan	607	−6	3.7	4
6.法国France	573	0	3.5	6
7.中国香港HongKong,SAR	547	−2	3.4	7
8.荷兰Netherlands	503	−2	3.4	8
9.加拿大Canada	417	−5	2.6	10
10.韩国Korea	406	−7	2.5	9

中国进出口总值

China's Total Value of Import & Export

单位：亿美元
Unit: USD 100 million

年度 Year	进出口 Import & Export	出口 Export	进口 Import	差额 Balance
1981	440	220	220	0
1982	416	223	193	30
1983	436	222	214	8
1984	535	261	274	−13
1985	696	274	423	−149
1986	738	309	429	−120
1987	827	394	432	−38
1988	1 028	475	553	−78
1989	1 117	525	591	−66
1990	1 154	621	534	87
1991	1 357	719	638	81
1992	1 655	849	806	44
1993	1 957	917	1 040	−122
1994	2 366	1 210	1 156	54
1995	2 809	1 488	1 321	167
1996	2 899	1 511	1 388	122
1997	3 252	1 828	1 424	404
1998	3 239	1 837	1 402	435
1999	3 606	1 949	1 657	292
2000	4 743	2 492	2 251	241
2001	5 097	2 661	2 436	226
2002	6 208	3 256	2 952	304
2003	8 510	4 382	4 128	255
2004	11 546	5 933	5 612	321
2005	14 219	7 620	6 600	1 020
2006	17 604	9 689	7 915	1 775
2007	21 766	12 205	9 561	2 643
2008	25 633	14 307	11 326	2 981
2009	22 072	12 017	10 059	1 957
2010	29 728	15 779	13 948	1 831
2011	36 421	18 986	17 435	1 551
2012	38 668	20 489	18 178	2 311
2013	41 603	22 100	19 503	2 598
2014	43 030	23 427	19 603	3 825
2015	39 569	22 749	16 820	5 930
2016	36 856	20 976	15 879	5 097

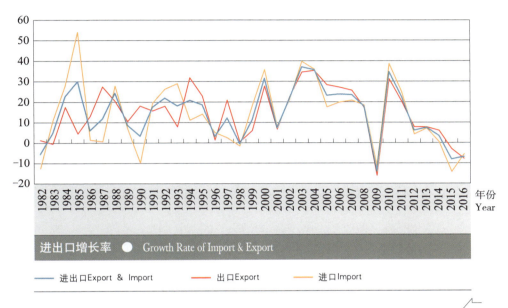

进出口增长率 ● Growth Rate of Import & Export

— 进出口Export ＆ Import　　— 出口Export　　— 进口Import

增长率 (%)
Growth Rate (%)

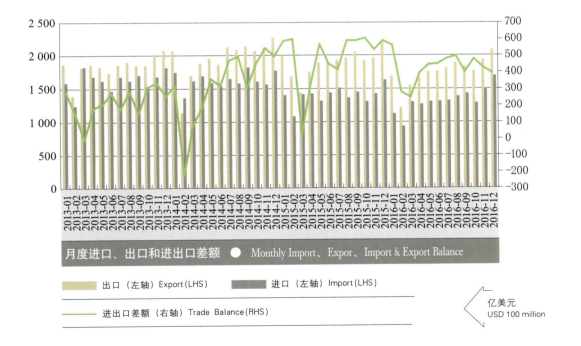

月度进口、出口和进出口差额 ● Monthly Import、Expor、Import & Export Balance

出口（左轴）Export (LHS)　　进口（左轴）Import (LHS)

— 进出口差额（右轴）Trade Balance(RHS)

亿美元
USD 100 million

按贸易方式分类进出口

Import & Export by Trading Forms

贸易方式Trading Forms	2006	2007	2008	2009	2010	2011	2012	2013	2014	2015	2016
进口Import	**791 614**	**955 818**	**1 133 086**	**1 005 555**	**1 394 829**	**1 743 458**	**1 817 826**	**1 950 289**	**1 960 290**	**1 681 951**	**1 587 921**
一般贸易Ordinary Trade	333 181	428 648	572 677	533 872	767 978	1 007 464	1 021 819	1 109 718	1 109 513	923 188	899 013
国家间、国际组织间无偿援助和捐赠的物资 Foreign Aid and Donation by Overseas	65	35	49	43	22	16	27	21	38	15	19
其他捐赠物资 Other Donations	22	10	58	136	185	266	338	11	10	48	8
来料加工装配贸易 Processing and Assembling Trade	73 834	89 165	90 162	75 993	99 295	93 635	84 459	87 543	97 537	91 569	85 261
进料加工贸易 Processing with Imported Materials	247 662	279 228	288 243	246 345	318 134	376 161	396 710	409 447	426 843	355 434	311 432
寄售代销贸易 Goods on Consignment	3	2	2	2	2	2	1	0	0		0
边境小额贸易 Border trade	6 214	7 589	8 975	7 196	9 634	14 448	15 289	14 065	9 856	7 160	7 019
加工贸易进口设备 Equipment Imported for Processing & Assembling	2 817	3 277	2 859	953	1 212	885	912	969	687	635	463
租赁贸易 Goods on Lease	8 067	8 280	6 932	3 448	5 628	5 459	6 760	8 656	10 212	9 041	2 860
外商投资企业作为投资进口的设备物品 Equipment or Materials Imported as Investment by Foreign-invested Enterprises	27 823	25 906	27 677	15 176	16 312	17 508	13 429	9 835	9 059	6 161	4 067
出料加工贸易 Outward Processing Trade	33	39	160	78	126	73	236	252	307	300	265
易货贸易 Barter Trade	6	4	1	8	1	2	0	1	3	3	8
免税外汇商品 Duty Free Commodities on Payment of Foreign Exchange	6	6	6	5	10	13	26	28	20	15	22
保税监管场所进出境货物 Customs Warehousing Trade	32 018	41 720	57 277	54 392	61 099	79 658	83 969	84 844	99 870	88 705	96 773
海关特殊监管区域物流货物 Entrepot Trade by Bonded Area	55 508	66 910	73 739	64 259	109 241	140 831	185 132	218 448	186 689	182 004	158 044
海关特殊监管区域进口设备 Equipment Imported into Export Processing Zone	3 623	4 108	3 118	2 113	3 994	4 741	6 094	3 993	5 133	6 544	4 894
其他 Others	732	890	1 150	1 535	1 957	2 296	2 624	2 458	2 950	9 510	15 542

单位：百万美元
Unit: USD million

贸易方式Trading Forms	2006	2007	2008	2009	2010	2011	2012	2013	2014	2015	2016
出口Export	**969 073**	**1 218 015**	**1 428 546**	**1 201 663**	**1 577 932**	**1 898 600**	**2 048 935**	**2 210 042**	**2 342 747**	**2 274 950**	**2 097 637**
一般贸易 Ordinary Trade	416 318	538 576	662 584	529 833	720 733	917 124	988 007	1 087 553	1 203 682	1 215 697	1 131 043
国家间、国际组织间无偿援助和捐赠的物资 Foreign Aid and Donation by overseas	211	201	231	291	294	471	551	456	478	493	472
其他捐赠物资 Other Donations	0	0	2	8	3	11	2	8	6	6	6
补偿贸易 Compensation Trade	1	0	0	0	0	0	0	0	0	0	0
来料加工装配贸易 Processing and Assembling Trade	94 483	116 043	110 520	93 423	112 317	107 653	98 866	92 479	90 692	84 097	76 040
进料加工贸易 Processing with Imported Materials	415 892	501 613	564 663	493 558	628 017	727 763	763 913	768 337	793 668	713 692	639 557
寄售代销贸易 Goods on Consignment	2	4	4	6	1	2	4	1	0	0	0
边境小额贸易 Border trade	9 943	13 739	21 904	13 667	16 408	20 203	24 216	30 929	37 207	30 465	26 407
对外承包工程出口货物 Contracting Projects	3 071	5 188	10 963	13 357	12 617	14 923	14 782	16 011	16 326	16 132	13 304
租赁贸易 Goods on Lease	214	84	189	117	145	166	562	305	327	265	192
出料加工贸易 Outward Processing Trade	24	44	118	46	185	198	196	199	235	205	221
易货贸易 Barter Trade	19	48	16	1	1	1	1	2	3	2	2
保税监管场所进出境货物 Customs Warehousing Trade	13 069	18 624	28 404	26 793	35 366	43 294	42 477	46 510	53 288	49 246	38 408
海关特殊监管区域物流货物 Entrepot Trade by Bonded Area	14 463	20 977	23 937	21 476	36 502	49 655	94 819	141 990	110 395	109 580	94 289
其他 Others	1 361	2 916	5 011	9 088	15 343	17 135	20 540	25 262	36 438	55 069	78 212

按企业类型分类进出口

Import & Export by Type of Enterprises

企业类型Type of Enterprises	2006	2007	2008	2009	2010	2011	2012	2013	2014	2015	2016
进口Import	**7 916**	**9 558**	**11 331**	**10 056**	**13 948**	**17 435**	**18 178**	**19 503**	**19 603**	**16 820**	**15 879**
国有企业State-owned Enterprises	2 252	2 697	3 538	2 885	3 876	4 934	4 954	4 990	4 911	4 078	3 608
外商投资企业 Foreign-funded Enterprises	4 726	5 594	6 200	5 452	7 380	8 648	8 712	8 748	9 093	8 299	7 705
中外合作 Sino-foreign Contractual Joint Ventures	99	88	88	66	74	86	82	83	87	62	43
中外合资 Sino-foreign Equity Joint Ventures	1 356	1 549	1 818	1 586	2 095	2 561	2 748	2 842	2 858	2 461	2 238
外商独资 Foreign Investment Enterprises	3 270	3 957	4 294	3 799	5 212	6 002	5 883	5 823	6 149	5 776	5 424
集体企业/私营企业① Collective Enterprises/Private owned Enterprises	200	232	289	265	349	407	353	4 368	4 475	4 116	4 179
其他Other Enterprises	738	1 035	1 304	1 454	2 343	3 445	4 158	1 397	1 124	326	375
出口Export	**9 691**	**12 180**	**14 285**	**12 017**	**15 779**	**18 986**	**20 489**	**22 100**	**23 427**	**22 749**	**20 976**
国有企业State-owned Enterprises	1 913	2 248	2 572	1 910	2 344	2 672	2 563	2 490	2 565	2 424	2 156
外商投资企业 Foreign-funded Enterprises	5 638	6 955	7 906	6 722	8 623	9 953	10 227	10 443	10 747	10 047	9 169
中外合作 Sino-foreign Contractual Joint Ventures	177	181	183	146	165	177	162	157	136	114	99
中外合资 Sino-foreign Equity Joint Ventures	1 638	1 988	2 269	1 824	2 376	2 731	2 873	3 009	3 055	2 825	2 542
外商独资 Foreign Investment Enterprises	3 824	4 786	5 454	4 752	6 082	7 046	7 193	7 277	7 556	7 109	6 529
集体企业/私营企业 Collective Enterprises/ Private owned Enterprises	411	469	547	405	499	554	509	8 633	9 547	9 738	9 148
其他Other Enterprises	1 728	2 508	3 260	2 979	4 314	5 807	7 190	534	958	541	503
差额Balance	**1 775**	**2 622**	**2 955**	**1 961**	**1 831**	**1 551**	**2 311**	**2 598**	**3 825**	**5 930**	**5 097**
国有企业State-owned Enterprises	−339	−449	−966	−975	−1 532	−2 262	−2 391	−2 500	−2 346	−1 654	−1 452
外商投资企业 Foreign-funded Enterprises	912	1 361	1 706	1 270	1 243	1 305	1 515	1 695	1 654	1 748	1 465
中外合作 Sino-foreign Contractual Joint Ventures	78	93	95	80	91	91	80	74	49	52	56
中外合资 Sino-foreign Equity Joint Ventures	281	439	451	238	281	170	125	167	197	364	304
外商独资 Foreign Investment Enterprises	553	829	1 160	953	870	1 044	1 310	1 454	1 407	1 333	1 105
集体企业/私营企业 Collective Enterprises/ Private owned Enterprises	211	237	258	140	150	147	156	4 265	5 072	5 622	4 968
其他Other Enterprises	990	1 473	1 956	1 525	1 971	2 362	3 032	−863	−166	214	128

① 2013 年该项下的数据由集体企业调整为私营企业。Data of Collective Enterprises was replaced by that of Private Owned Enterprises from 2013.

2016年按贸易方式分类的进口构成
Components of Import by Trading Forms in 2016

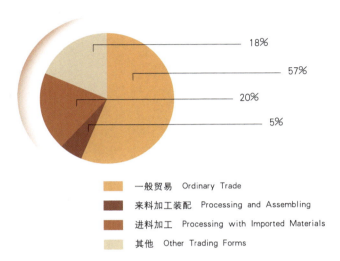

18%

57%

20%

5%

■ 一般贸易　Ordinary Trade

■ 来料加工装配　Processing and Assembling

■ 进料加工　Processing with Imported Materials

■ 其他　Other Trading Forms

2016年按贸易方式分类的出口构成
Components of Export by Trading Forms in 2016

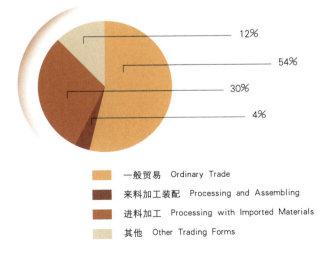

12%

54%

30%

4%

■ 一般贸易　Ordinary Trade

■ 来料加工装配　Processing and Assembling

■ 进料加工　Processing with Imported Materials

■ 其他　Other Trading Forms

2016年按企业类型分类的进口构成
Components of Import by Type of Enterprises in 2016

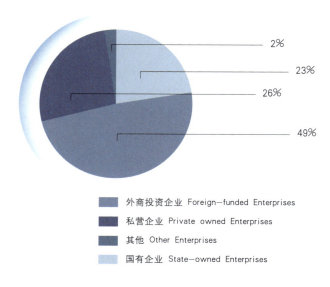

2%
23%
26%
49%

外商投资企业 Foreign-funded Enterprises
私营企业 Private owned Enterprises
其他 Other Enterprises
国有企业 State-owned Enterprises

2016年按企业类型分类的出口构成
Components of Export by Type of Enterprises in 2016

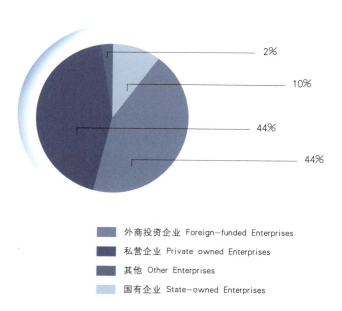

2%
10%
44%
44%

外商投资企业 Foreign-funded Enterprises
私营企业 Private owned Enterprises
其他 Other Enterprises
国有企业 State-owned Enterprises

2016年进出口按贸易方式分类

Import & Export by Trading Forms in 2016

单位：亿美元
Unit: USD 100 million

贸易方式 Trading Forms	进口 Import		出口 Export		进出口差额
	金额Value	同比（%）Increase	金额Value	同比（%）Increase	Import & Export Balance
总值 **Total Value**	**15 879**	**−5.5**	**20 976**	**−7.7**	**5 097**
一般贸易 Ordinary Trade	8 990	−2.5	11 310	−6.9	2 320
加工贸易 Processing Trade	3 967	−11.2	7 159	−10.2	3 192
来料加工装配 Processing and Assembling	853	−6.9	760	−9.6	−93
进料加工 Processing with imported materials	3 114	−12.3	6 396	−10.4	3 282
其他贸易 Other trading forms	2 917	−6.2	2 515	−3.3	−402

2016年进出口按企业类型分类

单位：亿美元
Unit: USD 100 million

Import & Export by Type of Enterprises in 2016

企业类型 Type of Enterprises	进口 Import		出口 Export		进出口差额
	金额Value	同比（%）Increase	金额Value	同比（%）Increase	Import & Export Balance
总值 **Total Value**	**15 879**	**−5.5**	**20 976**	**−7.7**	**5 097**
国有企业 State−owned Enterprises	3 608	−11.4	2 156	−11.0	−1 452
外资企业 Foreign−funded Enterprises	7 705	−7.1	9 169	−8.7	1 465
私营和其他企业 Private Owned and other Enterprises	4 555	2.8	9 651	−6.0	5 096

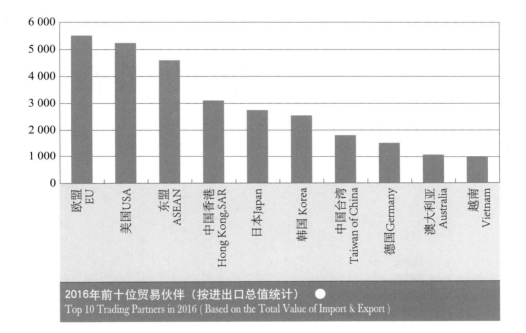

2016年前十位贸易伙伴（按进出口总值统计） ●
Top 10 Trading Partners in 2016（Based on the Total Value of Import & Export）

亿 美 元
USD 100 million

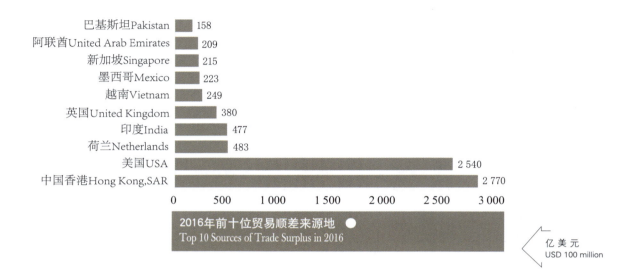

2016年前十位贸易顺差来源地
Top 10 Sources of Trade Surplus in 2016

亿 美 元
USD 100 million

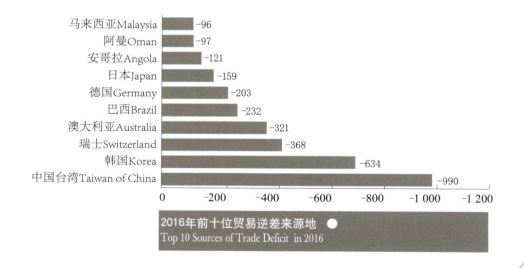

2016年前十位贸易逆差来源地
Top 10 Sources of Trade Deficit in 2016

亿 美 元
USD 100 million

三、外汇市场和人民币汇率[①]

Ⅲ. Foreign Exchange Market and Exchange Rate of RMB

人民币对美元交易中间价月平均汇价

人民币元/100美元
RMB per 100 USD

Monthly Average Transaction Mid Rates of Renminbi against USD, 1980—2016

年份Year 月份Month	1980	1981	1982	1983	1984	1985	1986	1987	1988	1989	1990
1 月/Jan.	149.37	154.87	176.77	192.01	204.12	280.88	320.15	372.21	372.21	372.21	472.21
2 月/Feb.	150.05	161.06	181.74	196.03	205.72	282.51	320.70	372.21	372.21	372.21	472.21
3 月/Mar.	155.12	162.80	183.79	197.80	206.08	284.51	321.20	372.21	372.21	372.21	472.21
4 月/Apr.	155.70	166.20	185.19	198.72	208.91	284.11	320.61	372.21	372.21	372.21	472.21
5 月/May	149.06	172.27	180.97	198.52	218.21	284.75	319.44	372.21	372.21	372.21	472.21
6 月/Jun.	146.50	176.05	189.70	198.95	221.22	286.25	320.35	372.21	372.21	372.21	472.21
7 月/Jul.	145.25	175.98	192.36	198.88	229.39	287.38	363.82	372.21	372.21	372.21	472.21
8 月/Aug.	147.26	179.52	193.87	198.00	236.43	290.23	370.36	372.21	372.21	372.21	472.21
9 月/Sept.	146.81	175.01	195.04	198.14	253.26	296.26	370.66	372.21	372.21	372.21	472.21
10 月/Oct.	148.03	175.05	198.22	196.17	264.00	306.73	371.64	372.21	372.21	372.21	472.21
11月/Nov.	151.73	173.46	199.41	198.90	266.16	320.15	372.21	372.21	372.21	372.21	495.54
12月/Dec.	154.19	173.78	193.99	198.69	278.91	320.15	372.21	372.21	372.21	423.82	522.21
年平均 Annual Average	149.84	170.50	189.25	197.57	232.70	293.66	345.28	372.21	372.21	376.51	478.32

---

①资料来源：国家外汇管理局。
Source: State Administration of Foreign Exchange.

人民币对美元交易中间价月平均汇价

人民币元/100美元
RMB per 100 USD

Monthly Average Transaction Mid Rates of Renminbi against USD, 1980—2016

年份Year 月份Month	1991	1992	1993	1994	1995	1996	1997	1998	1999	2000	2001	2002	2003
1 月/Jan.	522.21	544.81	576.40	870.00	844.13	831.86	829.63	827.91	827.90	827.93	827.71	827.67	827.68
2 月/Feb.	522.21	546.35	576.99	870.28	843.54	831.32	829.29	827.91	827.80	827.79	827.70	827.66	827.73
3 月/Mar.	522.21	547.34	573.13	870.23	842.76	832.89	829.57	827.92	827.91	827.86	827.76	827.70	827.72
4 月/Apr.	526.59	549.65	570.63	869.55	842.25	833.15	829.57	827.92	827.92	827.93	827.71	827.72	827.71
5 月/May	531.39	550.36	572.17	866.49	831.28	832.88	829.29	827.90	827.85	827.77	827.72	827.69	827.69
6 月/Jun.	535.35	547.51	573.74	865.72	830.08	832.26	829.21	827.97	827.80	827.72	827.71	827.70	827.71
7 月/Jul.	535.55	544.32	576.12	864.03	830.07	831.60	829.11	827.98	827.77	827.93	827.69	827.68	827.73
8 月/Aug.	537.35	542.87	577.64	858.98	830.75	830.81	828.94	827.99	827.73	827.96	827.70	827.67	827.70
9 月/Sept.	537.35	549.48	578.70	854.03	831.88	830.44	828.72	827.89	827.74	827.86	827.68	827.70	827.71
10 月/Oct.	537.90	553.69	578.68	852.93	831.55	830.00	828.38	827.78	827.74	827.85	827.68	827.69	827.67
11月/Nov.	538.58	561.31	579.47	851.69	831.35	829.93	828.11	827.78	827.82	827.74	827.69	827.71	827.69
12月/Dec.	541.31	579.82	580.68	848.45	831.56	829.90	827.96	827.79	827.93	827.72	827.68	827.72	827.70
年平均 Annual Average	532.33	551.46	576.20	861.87	835.10	831.42	828.98	827.91	827.83	827.84	827.70	827.70	827.70

人民币对美元交易中间价月平均汇价

人民币元/100美元
RMB per 100 USD

Monthly Average Transaction Mid Rates of Renminbi against USD，1980—2016

月份Month ＼ 年份Year	2004	2005	2006	2007	2008	2009	2010	2011	2012	2013	2014	2015	2016
1 月/Jan.	827.69	827.65	806.68	778.98	724.78	683.82	682.73	660.27	631.68	627.87	610.43	612.72	655.27
2 月/Feb.	827.71	827.65	804.93	775.46	716.01	683.57	682.70	658.31	630.00	628.42	611.28	613.39	653.11
3 月/Mar.	827.71	827.65	803.50	773.90	707.52	683.41	682.64	656.62	630.81	627.43	613.58	615.07	650.64
4 月/Apr.	827.69	827.65	801.56	772.47	700.07	683.12	682.62	652.92	629.66	624.71	615.53	613.02	647.62
5 月/May	827.71	827.65	801.52	767.04	697.24	682.45	682.74	649.88	630.62	619.70	616.36	611.43	653.15
6 月/Jun.	827.67	827.65	800.67	763.30	689.71	683.32	681.65	647.78	631.78	617.18	615.57	611.61	658.74
7 月/Jul.	827.67	822.90	799.10	758.05	683.76	683.20	677.75	646.14	632.35	617.25	615.69	611.67	667.74
8 月/Aug.	827.68	810.19	797.33	757.53	685.15	683.22	679.01	640.9	634.04	617.08	616.06	630.56	664.74
9 月/Sept.	827.67	809.22	793.68	752.58	683.07	682.89	674.62	638.33	633.95	615.88	615.28	636.91	667.15
10 月/Oct.	827.65	808.89	790.32	750.12	683.16	682.75	667.32	635.66	631.44	613.93	614.41	634.86	674.42
11月/Nov.	827.65	808.40	786.52	742.33	682.86	682.74	665.58	634.08	629.53	613.72	614.32	636.66	683.75
12月/Dec.	827.65	807.59	782.38	736.76	684.24	682.79	665.15	632.81	629.00	611.60	612.38	644.76	691.82
年平均 Annual Average	827.68	819.42	797.18	760.40	694.51	683.10	676.95	646.14	631.25	619.32	614.28	622.72	664.23

2016年1—12月人民币市场汇率汇总表

美元、港币、日元、欧元、英镑、澳元、新西兰元、新加坡元、瑞士法郎、加元10种币种单位为人民币元/100外币，其他币种单位为外币/100人民币
USD、HKD、JPY、EUR、GBP、AUD、NZD、CHF、CAD Unit: foreign currency per 100 renminbi Other Currency unit:renminbi per 100 foreign currency

Transaction Mid Rates of Renminbi in 2016

月份Month	币种 Currency	期初价 Beginning of Period	期末价 End of Period	最高价 Highest	最低价 Lowest	期平均 Period Average	累计平均 Accumulative Average
1月 Jan.	美元	650.32	655.16	656.46	650.32	655.27	655.27
	港币	83.906	84.091	84.680	83.865	84.231	84.231
	日元	5.3993	5.5205	5.6163	5.3993	5.5531	5.5531
	欧元	704.83	717.00	719.36	701.30	712.45	712.45
	英镑	957.27	942.09	961.25	929.87	945.60	945.60
	澳元	473.29	464.91	473.29	450.80	460.17	460.17
	新西兰元	442.69	425.00	442.69	419.46	428.92	428.92
	新加坡元	457.47	459.84	460.24	456.26	457.91	457.91
	加元	649.37	646.81	663.05	645.19	652.12	652.12
	林吉特	468.97	466.60	468.97	450.06	460.92	460.92
	卢布	66.201	63.458	67.405	63.458	66.087	66.087
2月 Feb.	美元	655.39	654.52	655.39	651.18	653.11	654.31
	港币	84.206	84.186	84.221	83.612	83.944	84.103
	日元	5.4112	5.7630	5.8312	5.4112	5.6770	5.6082
	欧元	710.75	715.33	733.97	710.75	722.32	716.83
	英镑	934.80	907.77	956.41	907.77	932.55	939.80
	澳元	463.46	466.51	472.93	460.83	467.17	463.28
	新西兰元	424.53	432.14	441.08	424.53	433.15	430.80
	新加坡元	460.24	464.56	468.45	458.84	464.13	460.68
	加元	641.61	657.24	668.74	641.61	655.58	653.66
	林吉特	468.37	482.86	482.86	465.05	473.80	466.65
	卢布	63.139	64.344	64.351	62.677	63.824	65.081
3月 Mar.	美元	653.85	646.12	654.90	646.12	650.64	652.88
	港币	84.114	83.325	84.241	83.325	83.828	83.996
	日元	5.8208	5.7530	5.8208	5.7070	5.7627	5.6684
	欧元	712.11	733.12	733.27	711.21	723.43	719.41
	英镑	911.59	929.35	937.18	911.59	925.94	934.40
	澳元	466.25	495.50	495.50	466.25	486.87	472.48
	新西兰元	431.93	446.79	446.79	430.62	437.84	433.54
	新加坡元	465.56	478.84	479.10	465.56	473.48	465.67
	加元	655.61	669.89	671.60	652.40	661.83	656.84
	林吉特	482.83	498.05	498.05	482.83	491.39	476.29
	卢布	63.785	60.775	63.785	60.775	62.479	64.067

2016年1—12月人民币市场汇率汇总表

美元、港币、日元、欧元、英镑、澳元、新西兰元、新加坡元、瑞士法郎、加元10种币种单位为人民币元/100外币，其他币种单位为外币/100人民币

USD、HKD、JPY、EUR、GBP、AUD、NZD、CHF、CAD Unit: foreign currency per 100 renminbi
Other Currency unit:renminbi per 100 foreign currency

Transaction Mid Rates of Renminbi in 2016

月份Month	币种 Currency	期初价 Beginning of Period	期末价 End of Period	最高价 Highest	最低价 Lowest	期平均 Period Average	累计平均 Accumulative Average
4月 Apr.	美元	645.85	645.89	651.20	645.79	647.62	651.55
	港币	83.280	83.257	83.953	83.257	83.496	83.870
	日元	5.7413	5.9820	5.9907	5.7413	5.9021	5.7276
	欧元	734.93	734.39	738.03	730.56	733.97	723.09
	英镑	927.74	944.03	945.32	910.20	926.34	932.36
	澳元	495.47	492.89	509.01	486.40	496.42	478.54
	新西兰元	446.88	449.64	453.66	439.23	446.04	436.71
	新加坡元	479.06	481.06	482.36	475.78	479.57	469.19
	加元	671.82	668.54	677.85	659.33	670.68	660.35
	林吉特	497.42	514.98	515.96	492.64	504.71	483.49
	卢布	60.021	59.935	60.486	59.608	59.985	63.034
5月 May	美元	645.65	657.90	657.90	645.65	653.15	651.88
	港币	83.210	84.685	84.700	83.210	84.128	83.924
	日元	6.0789	5.9320	6.0917	5.9320	5.9980	5.7844
	欧元	744.76	733.18	747.65	730.15	738.25	726.28
	英镑	947.91	963.26	963.68	937.66	948.73	935.79
	澳元	495.64	473.15	495.64	470.97	477.69	478.36
	新西兰元	454.80	441.26	454.80	439.81	444.06	438.25
	新加坡元	482.38	476.77	482.38	474.41	476.68	470.76
	加元	676.92	663.46	680.88	660.75	667.69	661.89
	林吉特	515.74	504.41	515.74	497.89	504.50	487.90
	卢布	60.192	62.319	62.345	60.192	61.651	62.743
6月 Jun.	美元	658.89	663.12	665.28	654.97	658.74	653.03
	港币	84.789	85.467	85.736	84.316	84.862	84.080
	日元	5.9543	6.4491	6.5300	5.9543	6.2436	5.8609
	欧元	733.08	737.50	745.63	731.84	739.83	728.54
	英镑	953.69	892.12	972.42	879.92	936.70	935.95
	澳元	476.90	494.52	495.51	475.32	486.86	479.78
	新西兰元	447.07	471.73	473.54	447.07	462.48	442.29
	新加坡元	478.03	492.39	492.39	477.29	486.25	473.34
	瑞士法郎	663.11	677.30	685.63	663.11	678.76	664.70
	加元	503.55	512.22	514.83	502.51	510.16	491.61
	林吉特	62.341	60.508	62.965	60.508	61.773	62.581
	卢布	1 010.50	960.75	1 019.24	960.75	989.86	1 071.47

2016年1—12月人民币市场汇率汇总表

林吉特、卢布单位：外币/100人民币
其他9种币种单位：人民币元/100外币
MYR, RUB Unit: foreign currency per 100 RMB
Other 9 Currency unit: RMB per 100 foreign currency

Transaction Mid Rates of Renminbi in 2016

月份Month	币种 Currency	期初价 Beginning of Period	期末价 End of Period	最高价 Highest	最低价 Lowest	期平均 Period Average	累计平均 Accumulative Average
7月 Jul.	美元	664.96	665.11	669.71	664.72	667.74	655.22
	港币	85.700	85.751	86.360	85.682	86.084	84.379
	日元	6.4457	6.3554	6.6350	6.2376	6.4183	5.9439
	欧元	737.96	737.24	742.26	732.73	738.47	730.02
	英镑	886.87	875.13	892.58	862.48	877.92	927.30
	澳元	495.23	499.75	508.86	495.23	502.15	483.11
	新西兰元	474.41	471.84	487.64	466.11	475.78	447.28
	新加坡元	493.63	492.04	497.49	490.24	494.28	476.46
	瑞士法郎	680.99	678.81	685.84	672.01	679.82	666.95
	加元	513.07	505.79	517.73	504.71	512.24	494.68
	林吉特	60.125	60.960	61.049	58.850	59.976	62.193
	卢布	960.17	1 002.34	1 002.34	937.77	962.57	1 055.25
8月 Aug.	美元	662.77	669.08	669.08	660.56	664.74	656.55
	港币	85.432	86.250	86.250	85.185	85.707	84.565
	日元	6.4716	6.5035	6.6404	6.4716	6.5633	6.0308
	欧元	740.98	746.02	753.79	738.16	744.87	732.10
	英镑	876.12	875.78	885.38	854.37	871.39	919.46
	澳元	503.37	503.29	511.57	500.26	506.89	486.44
	新西兰元	477.37	484.25	487.49	474.09	480.42	451.93
	新加坡元	494.46	490.61	495.33	490.61	493.52	478.85
	瑞士法郎	683.96	680.74	693.56	677.70	684.82	669.46
	加元	507.77	510.55	517.66	504.79	511.45	497.03
	林吉特	60.927	60.407	60.927	59.929	60.388	61.940
	卢布	997.43	974.70	1008.12	960.83	977.92	1 044.41
9月 Sep.	美元	667.84	667.78	669.08	665.13	667.15	657.71
	港币	86.097	86.097	86.256	85.766	86.014	84.722
	日元	6.4678	6.6012	6.6421	6.4345	6.5509	6.0873
	欧元	745.60	748.80	751.61	743.83	747.74	733.80
	英镑	877.65	865.46	893.56	864.16	877.36	914.89
	澳元	502.48	509.24	513.21	500.11	506.77	488.65
	新西兰元	483.99	483.75	496.78	482.95	487.76	455.82
	新加坡元	490.26	488.94	494.79	488.26	491.18	480.19
	瑞士法郎	679.13	691.08	691.08	679.13	684.85	571.13
	加元	509.35	507.37	517.74	502.42	510.07	498.45
	林吉特	60.909	61.675	61.917	60.654	61.337	61.875
	卢布	977.84	945.86	987.29	945.40	965.66	1 035.85

2016年1—12月人民币市场汇率汇总表

林吉特、卢布单位：外币/100人民币
其他7种币种单位：人民币元/100外币
MYR, RUB Unit: foreign currency per 100 RMB
Other 7 Currency unit: RMB per 100 foreign currency

Transaction Mid Rates of Renminbi in 2016

月份Month	币种 Currency	期初价 Beginning of Period	期末价 End of Period	最高价 Highest	最低价 Lowest	期平均 Period Average	累计平均 Accumulative Average
10月 Dot.	美元	670.08	676.41	678.58	670.08	674.42	659.04
	港币	86.372	87.225	87.506	86.372	86.937	84.900
	日元	6.4964	6.4631	6.5137	6.4518	6.4842	6.1191
	欧元	748.94	742.94	748.94	736.04	740.59	734.34
	英镑	832.01	825.01	832.01	819.82	825.75	907.75
	澳元	508.71	513.73	519.51	507.81	513.47	490.64
	新西兰元	480.06	484.04	486.92	473.95	481.66	457.89
	新加坡元	487.17	486.33	488.16	483.95	486.24	480.68
	瑞士法郎	684.45	684.95	684.95	679.69	681.58	671.97
	加元	506.12	504.22	514.33	504.22	508.76	499.28
	林吉特	61.890	61.885	62.544	61.151	61.896	61.876
	卢布	929.16	931.49	942.51	918.16	929.04	1 027.30
11月 Nov.	美元	677.34	688.65	691.68	674.91	683.75	661.49
	港币	87.343	88.794	89.179	87.028	88.157	85.222
	日元	6.4620	6.1316	6.5530	6.1058	6.3266	6.1396
	欧元	742.80	733.86	750.99	728.17	738.51	734.76
	英镑	828.53	860.85	861.41	827.03	849.85	902.02
	澳元	514.74	516.01	525.86	505.50	515.51	493.10
	新西兰元	484.42	491.93	500.27	483.10	489.08	460.98
	新加坡元	486.80	483.98	488.95	482.27	485.20	481.13
	瑞士法郎	684.81	681.46	696.29	679.42	686.94	673.45
	加元	504.65	513.32	513.93	503.97	508.78	500.22
	林吉特	61.731	64.569	64.569	61.542	63.053	61.993
	卢布	935.64	945.78	964.24	924.55	941.73	1 018.82
12月 Dec.	美元	689.58	693.70	695.08	685.75	691.82	664.23
	港币	88.910	89.451	89.583	88.425	89.164	85.578
	日元	6.0351	5.9591	6.0792	5.8809	5.9692	6.1243
	欧元	731.11	730.68	739.53	722.70	729.25	734.26
	英镑	864.29	850.94	874.17	850.94	863.56	898.55
	澳元	510.21	501.57	517.31	498.52	508.20	494.46
	新西兰元	488.87	483.08	497.22	478.10	486.83	463.31
	新加坡元	481.47	479.95	485.36	479.18	481.96	481.20
	瑞士法郎	678.88	679.89	682.64	675.25	678.60	673.92
	加元	514.37	514.06	526.71	512.10	518.50	501.87
	林吉特	64.665	64.406	64.665	63.826	64.250	62.197
	卢布	929.97	869.06	931.44	869.06	896.94	1 007.83

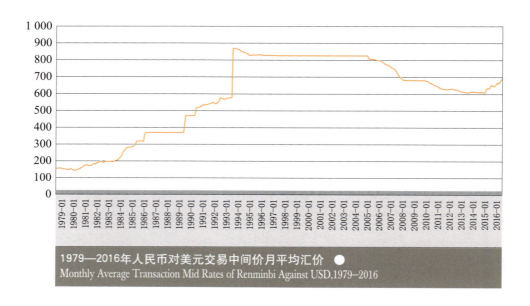

1979—2016年人民币对美元交易中间价月平均汇价 ●
Monthly Average Transaction Mid Rates of Renminbi Against USD,1979—2016

人民币元/100美元
RMB per 100 USD

四、利用外资①

Ⅳ. Foreign Investment Utilization

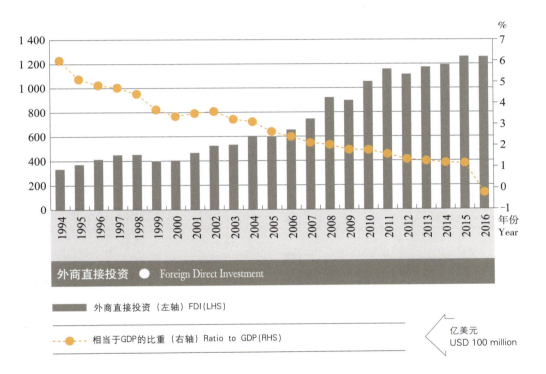

①资料来源：商务部。
Source: Ministry of Commerce.

2016年利用外资

Foreign Direct Investment in 2016

单位：亿美元
Unit: USD 100 million

利用外资方式 Mode of Foreign Investment Utilization	本年批准外资项目数 Approved Foreign Investment Programs		本年实际使用外资 Actual Utilization of Foreign Investment	
	本年累计 Accumulative in This Year	同比增长(%) Increase	本年累计 Accumulative in This Year	同比增长(%) Increase
总计 Total	27 900	5.0	1 260	−0.2
一、外商直接投资 Direct Foreign Investment	27 900	5.0	1 260	−0.2
中外合资企业 Sino–Foreign Equity Joint Venture	6 662	11.2	302	16.7
中外合作企业 Sino–Foreign Contractual Joint Venture	126	14.6	8.3	−55.0
外资企业 Foreign Investment Enterprise	21 024	3.1	861.3	−9.6
外商投资股份制 Stock–Holding by Foreign Investment	86	10.3	88.4	172.0
合作开发Cooperation Exploitation	0	0.0	0	0.0
其他 Others	0	0.0	0	0.0
二、外商其他投资 Other Foreign Investment	0	0.0	0	0.0
对外发行股票 Issue Stocks to the Outside	0	0.0	0	0.0
国际租赁 International Tenancy	0	0.0	0	0.0
补偿贸易Compensative Trade	0	0.0	0	0.0
加工装配 Processing & Assembling	0	0.0	0	0.0

注：统计数据为非金融领域。
Note: The data is subject to non–financial sectors.

五、外债①

V. External Debt

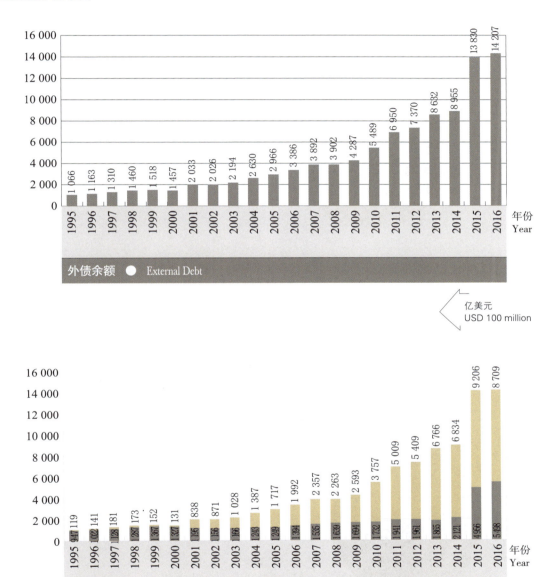

外债余额 ● External Debt

外债余额期限结构（剩余期限）●
Components of External Debt by Period Structure (Residual Maturity)

■ 中长期外债余额 Long and Medium-term External Debt

□ 短期外债余额 Short-term External Debt

亿美元
USD 100 million

① 数据来源：国家外汇管理局。
Source: State Administration of Foreign Exchange.

2016年末外债余额期限结构（剩余期限）
Components of External Debt by Period Structure (Residual Maturity), End—2016

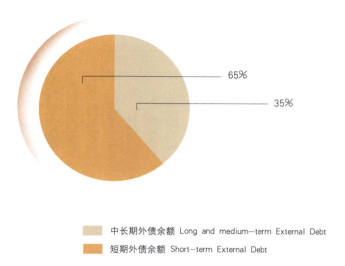

65%

35%

中长期外债余额 Long and medium—term External Debt
短期外债余额 Short—term External Debt

2016年末登记外债余额主体结构
Components of Registered External Debt by Type of Debtor, End—2016

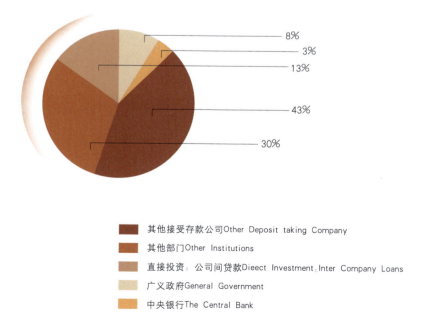

8%
3%
13%
43%
30%

其他接受存款公司Other Deposit taking Company
其他部门Other Institutions
直接投资：公司间贷款Dieect Investment：Inter Company Loans
广义政府General Government
中央银行The Central Bank

六、世界经济增长状况①

Ⅵ. Growth of World Economy

世界主要经济体增长率 ● Growth Rate of Major Economies in the World

- ◆- 中国 China ┈■┈ 美国 USA -▲- 欧元区 Euro Area —●— 日本 Japan

注：美国、日本和欧元区是实际GDP季比折年增速，中国为年比增速。
Note: The growth rates of U.S., Japan and Euro Area are the annualized quarterly growth rates, and the growth rate of China is the year-on-year quarterly growth rate.

经济增长率 (%)
Growth Rate of Economy (%)

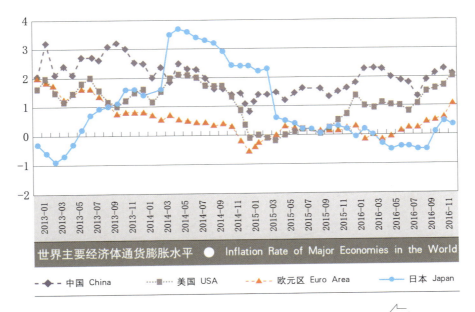

世界主要经济体通货膨胀水平 ● Inflation Rate of Major Economies in the World

- ◆- 中国 China ┈■┈ 美国 USA -▲- 欧元区 Euro Area —●— 日本 Japan

居民消费价格指数
CPI

①资料来源：彭博资讯；CEIC Asia Database。
Sources: Bloomberg, CEIC Asia Database.

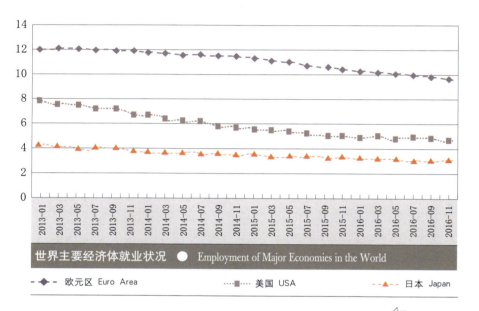

世界主要经济体就业状况 ● Employment of Major Economies in the World

- ◆- 欧元区 Euro Area　　　……■…… 美国 USA　　　-▲- 日本 Japan

失业率 (%)
Unemployment Rate (%)

七、国际金融市场状况^①

Ⅶ. International Financial Market

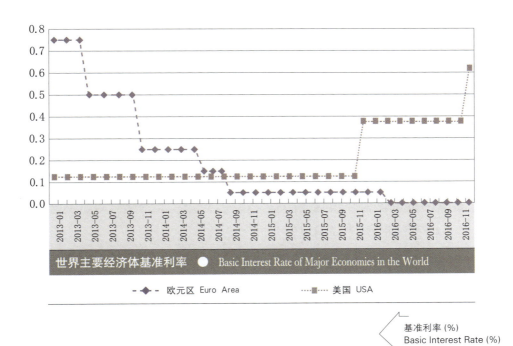

世界主要经济体基准利率　●　Basic Interest Rate of Major Economies in the World

- ◆ - 欧元区 Euro Area　　……■…… 美国 USA

基准利率 (%)
Basic Interest Rate (%)

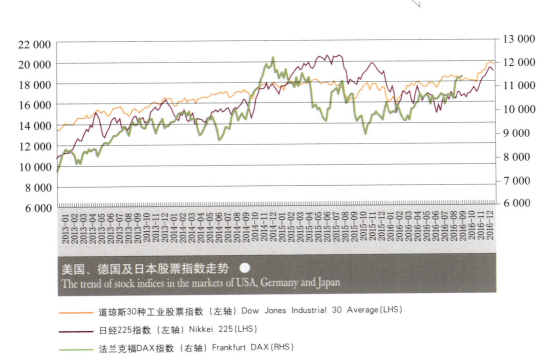

美国、德国及日本股票指数走势　●
The trend of stock indices in the markets of USA, Germany and Japan

—— 道琼斯30种工业股票指数（左轴）Dow Jones Industrial 30 Average(LHS)
—— 日经225指数（左轴）Nikkei 225(LHS)
—— 法兰克福DAX指数（右轴）Frankfurt DAX(RHS)

①资料来源：彭博资讯。
Source: Bloomberg.

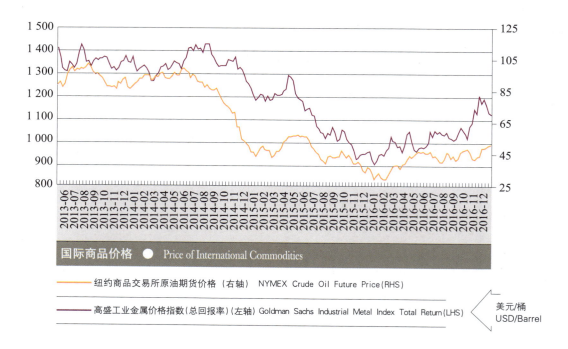

国际商品价格 ● Price of International Commodities

———— 纽约商品交易所原油期货价格（右轴） NYMEX Crude Oil Future Price（RHS）

———— 高盛工业金属价格指数（总回报率）（左轴）Goldman Sachs Industrial Metal Index Total Return（LHS）

美元/桶
USD/Barrel

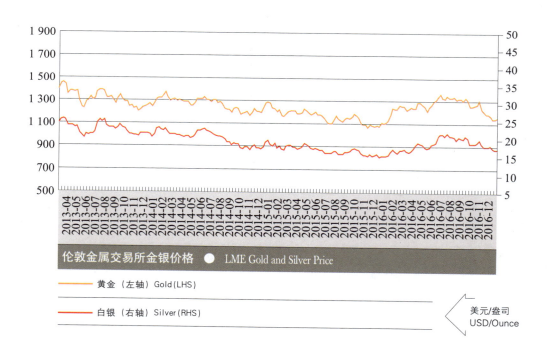

伦敦金属交易所金银价格 ● LME Gold and Silver Price

———— 黄金（左轴）Gold（LHS）

———— 白银（右轴）Silver（RHS）

美元/盎司
USD/Ounce